★ ★ ★ ★ ★ ★

Allah

THE GOD OF ISLAM

MOSLEM LIFE AND WORSHIP

★

by

Florence Mary Fitch

★

Illustrated with photographs
Selected by
Beatrice Creighton and
the author

LOTHROP, LEE & SHEPARD CO., INC. • NEW YORK

31305
1/29/58

Juv
BP
161
.F5
1950

Second Printing, September, 1956

Allah

THE GOD OF ISLAM

There is no God but Allah,
and Mohammed is his Prophet

THE WORLD OF ISLAM

FIVE TIMES a day three hundred million people, bowing in prayer, turn their faces toward Mecca, a small oasis town in the vast Arabian desert. This was the home of Mohammed, whose life and teaching are the heart of Islam. This is still the religious center of the Moslem world.

Islam, which means submission to God, and includes the life and culture as well as the religion, is better known to outsiders as Mohammedanism. Its followers, however, object to that name; they say that they do not worship Mohammed as Christians and Buddhists worship Christ and Buddha; they worship only Allah, the One God.

Islam began in Arabia in the seventh century A.D. and within a hundred years its rulers controlled an empire more vast than that of Rome. Within four hundred years it was the treasure-house of the richest culture of the world. This is the miracle of Islam.

Today the Middle East, where Islam began, is the focus of world interest. It is the meeting point of three continents; whoever controls it, controls the highways of the eastern hemisphere. Britain, Russia and the United States are concerned about its resources and seek the friendship of its governments. The Jewish people are working to reestablish their homeland there. The relatively weak Arab states are stirring with national ambitions and hopes. The Middle East has come to life again and is in ferment; and in the center is Islam.

Islam is one of the most democratic and vital religions of the world, the faith of one seventh of the human race. The three hundred million believers, who call themselves Moslems, live in countries that extend from the west coast of Africa to the islands of the Pacific; they are found also in Europe and the Americas. They include all races, nationalities, tongues, and colors, and all stages of culture; yet they are bound together by a common faith and a common way of life.

HE WORLD OF ISLAM

The royal family of Saudi Arabia are loyal Moslems
who live by the teachings of Mohammed.

A servant on the estate faces Mecca at the hour of prayer, as does every other Moslem wherever he may be.

Moslems gather in a street in the Kasbah to drink a cup of coffee and exchange the news.

Children of the Kasbah are like children the world over. The little boy is getting ready to jump from the doorway to impress his sister.

Moslems in India celebrate a religious festival.

Egyptian Moslems passing the pyramids on their way to a desert wedding.

This small Moslem scholar is a valued employee in a silk plant in Kashmir. He is sent to classes for a brief period each day to learn to read and to copy the Koran.

An old man from Burma has just completed his journey of thousands of miles to make the pilgrimage to Mecca, expected of every Moslem once in his lifetime.

This young Arabian, an interpreter for Americans in his country, is learning to understand America, too.

The wives and relatives of a wealthy Moslem in Tunis are taking their daily exercise. Their bulky clothes are worn as protection against the heat.

Modern Arab farm laborers enjoying their morning coffee. When coffee was first introduced into Arabia, the Meccans became so fond of it that they established the first known coffee-houses, the Kaveh Khanehs.

Arabia is the date center of the world and many young Moslem girls as well as men are employed during the harvest.

Turkish family enjoying a favorite Moslem game. The ivory chess set with its realistic figures came from China; those made in Moslem lands would not have human or animal figures because Mohammed forbade making "any likeness of any living thing."

The Shah of Persia rules over a country whose national religion is Islam. Persia is rapidly becoming a modern nation but it still prizes the culture of its glorious past and still follows the leadership of Mohammed.

MOHAMMED, THE FOUNDER OF ISLAM

IN THE STORY of Mohammed's life, facts, traditions, and legends are hard to separate. His father died shortly before his birth in Mecca in 571 A.D. When his mother died a few years later, he was left to the care of his grandfather and his uncle. Like other Arab boys he began early to herd sheep. Years of solitude made him observant and thoughtful. There were no schools in that country at that time; an eager boy learned where and what he could.

Mecca was a thrilling place in which to grow up, for it is the most sacred place in all Arabia. Here is "the black stone," believed to have fallen from Paradise. Long before the time of Mohammed, when the Arabs worshiped many gods and when stones were held sacred, this black stone had been built into the wall of the Ka'aba, a square stone structure. Around this were shrines with idols of many deities.

Twice a year, at the religious festivities, Mecca thronged with pilgrims. Poets and singers vied with one another in praise of their tribes, their patrons, and their gods. Neighboring bedouin came with their wool and their fruits, their spices and textiles. Caravans, with gold and ivory from Egypt, dates and perfume from the southland, grain and olives from the north, and even silks from India, rested in this welcome oasis, traded and enjoyed themselves. In Mecca's crowded streets, nomads and city dwellers met.

When Mohammed was twelve years old, he made his first long journey in a caravan with his uncle. They traveled into northern Syria and came in touch with cultures and people unlike any the boy had known. He returned home more thoughtful than ever.

Several years later, Khadijah, the widow of a wealthy merchant, hired him as leader of her caravan. She was so satisfied that she asked him to marry her, although he was fifteen years younger than she was. In this happy marriage Khadijah bore two sons, who died in infancy, and four daughters. Although daughters were not highly valued by Arabs, tradition says that Mohammed was often seen playing with his little daughters, "smelling" them—the oriental substitute for kissing. Only one of them, Fatima, survived her father; their love for each other has made the name of Fatima a highly honored one. Two grandsons, Hasan and Husein, he called his two precious plants, the chief treasures of his life.

Arab bedouin today live as they did in the time of Mohammed, pitching their tents wherever their sheep can find grass.

Like this Arab boy, Mohammed was taught to listen to his elders.

Between trading trips, Mohammed gave much time to solitary thought and talked often with the more earnest men of the town. Among them were Jews and Christians, who, because of persecution or for purposes of trade, were living in Mecca. Doubtless he attended services in synagogue and church and listened to stories read from the scriptures. He learned of the One God of all the world, who had revealed Himself to His chosen people through His prophets from the time of righteous Abraham to the time of His servant Jesus. He heard high ideals of justice and mercy and honesty; he saw the worshipers engaging in prayer and chant. He found that the One God had made known His will in a Book, that He had brought punishment even upon His chosen ones when they did not obey, and that He would yet bring judgment upon the whole world for its sins. All this gave Mohammed a sense of impending doom. Sometimes he attended public discussions in which Jews and Christians of various opinions argued about their beliefs and practices. He knew some Arabs who, influenced by contacts with Jews and Christians, had given up worship of many gods and believed only in Allah—THE God.

Mohammed began to spend many hours, sometimes days and weeks in a little cave on Mt. Hira, a hill near Mecca, as he had seen Christian hermits do in the cave-studded hills of Syria. Arab writers tell how he endured long fasts and night vigils. Alone with his own soul in the silence of the vast desert, he wrestled with questions which face all thoughtful men, questions about the meaning of things, the nature of the Divine Being or Beings, the destiny of man. One night near the end of the month Ramadan of his fortieth year, he was given the answer. He saw clearly what he had heard from Jews and Christians, that there is but one God, all other gods are mere idols, bits of stone. Men come and men go; one generation dies and another is born; but God endures. Man is truly free only as he submits to God and works with His supreme will.

Then Allah—God—spoke to him through Gabriel, the angel of revelation, who appeared and commanded: "Recite!" "I cannot," Mohammed replied. Gabriel gripped him tightly and repeated, "Recite!" Again he answered, "I cannot." When Gabriel gave the command the third time, he asked, "What shall I recite?" and the angel said:

> "Recite! in the name of the Lord,
> Who created man out of a clot of blood.
> Recite! for thy Lord is most gracious,
> Who taught by means of the pen,
> Taught man what he did not know."

Mohammed, still confused, fled to the top of the mountain and there, under the star-lit tropical sky, in the clear desert air, he heard a voice saying, "Thou art a prophet." Frightened and dazed, he hurried home to Khadijah and exclaimed, "Am I a prophet or am I mad?" She quieted and comforted him.

After this "Night of Power," as it was later named, Gabriel appeared to Mohammed again and told him that his mission was to restore to the Arabs the pure faith of their father Abraham and to free them from bondage to idolatry. The Arabs, sons of Abraham through Ishmael, even as the Jews were descended through Isaac, were to be the last link in the world-history which had been directed by God. After this Gabriel returned frequently to bring Mohammed the help he needed for each new problem.

At first Mohammed shared his revelation only with his own family and friends. His wife believed in him from the beginning, so did his cousin Ali. These two never failed in their loyal support. The first man outside of the household to believe in Mohammed was Abu Bekr, a highly esteemed and wealthy merchant. After three years Mohammed had won about thirty converts, most of them humble folk.

Now, as in Mohammed's day, ideas as well as produce are exchanged in the market place.

Then he began to preach in the market-place. At first they laughed good-humoredly, saying "There goes the man that always talks about religion." They thought him just another soothsayer. They knew many such popular seers, who ascribed their wisdom to supernatural powers and who also spoke in rhymed prose. But when his listeners began to understand his teaching, they arose in violent opposition. They were afraid Mohammed would keep away the visitors who came to the sacred shrine with its many gods and provided the chief income of the city, for Mohammed demanded belief in One God and complete submission to Him. He insisted that all those who did not believe would perish in everlasting fire; he consigned all ancestors, including his own, to unending torment. The citizens of Mecca, to whom loyalty to those bound by blood was the supreme point of honor, demanded that he be silenced. They asked his uncle to forbid his teaching such radical views, but when his uncle tried to dissuade him, Mohammed answered: "If they brought the sun to my right hand and the moon to my left to force me from my undertaking, I would not desist until the Lord makes manifest His cause or I perish in the attempt." His uncle stood by him and the family was ostracised.

After this Mohammed lived and worked in seclusion. He spoke publicly only at the festivals, when a "truce of God," an agreement among all the Arab tribes, insured that there would be no violence at the time of the pilgrimages.

During this period of discouragement, both his wife and his uncle died. Yet sorrow silenced him no more than ridicule or danger. One night, according to tradition, he had a dream which made him even more confident of his mission. In the dream Gabriel came and placed him upon Borak, a winged horse with a woman's face and a peacock's tail. Borak transported him to Jerusalem, where he met Abraham, Moses, and Jesus. Then he carried him to the Seventh Heaven, where he received revelations too wonderful to describe.

About this time Omar, a man of "blood and iron," determined to silence Mohammed by death. But when he stood before him his sword fell from his hand and he consecrated himself to the service of Allah. His conversion gave other Moslems courage; now they came out into the open, praying even at Mecca's holy shrine.

Many pilgrims who came to Mecca heard the teaching of Mohammed. Most of them went back to their free nomad life, untroubled by the warnings, but some were impressed. These returned the next year, bringing others. One such group from Medina, a city some three hundred miles north of Mecca, was so stirred that they invited Mohammed to make their city his home.

To break the connections with his family and his home-city and throw in his lot with strangers was unthinkable by Arab standards, and the Meccans were outraged when Mohammed accepted the invitation. Some two hundred of his companions decided to go with him. Divided into small groups, they slipped out of the city by stealth and began the eleven day journey on foot to Medina, with the hostile Meccans in pursuit. Mohammed and the devoted Abu Bekr were the last to leave. As they hid from their pursuers in a cave Abu Bekr said, "We two are alone," and Mohammed replied, "No, we are three; God is with us."

This was in the year 622 A.D., known as the year of the Hegira—the Flight. It marks the beginning of the Moslem Era; subtracting 622 from an A.D. date according to the Christian reckoning gives the corresponding Moslem date A.H. The migration to Medina marked a new era indeed; it was the beginning of Islam as an institution and as a state.

In Medina there were both Arab and Jewish tribes, constantly at strife among themselves. The companions who had come with Mohammed formed still another group. Mohammed wanted to win all these different factions to Islam and make the bonds of religion closer than any ties of race or tribe. He drew up a constitution to unite them in a single community; they were to protect one another against all foes, assist one another in all difficulties, and refer all cases of disagreement to God and His Prophet.

What seemed a simple reform was in reality a revolution. The separate tribes surrendered their power to the state. Mohammed, the astute politician, had gained absolute authority for himself. He was ruler, law-giver, judge, and military commander, as well as prophet. Whatever he thought necessary for the life of the community was the divine will. When his conduct was questioned, he justified it by reporting a special divine revelation.

Mohammed hoped that the Jews of Medina would support him, for he believed that his religion was at heart the same as theirs. He allowed them political equality and full freedom of worship. He taught his followers to face toward Jerusalem when they prayed as the Jews did and to observe the Jewish fasts. But the Jews refused to acknowledge him as a prophet, even taunted him with the errors he made in repeating the Old Testament stories. Yet this did not shake his own faith in his mission.

Mohammed never lost sight of his goal, to unite all of his countrymen in the true faith. When persuasion did not succeed with the Jews, he gave

Arabs have always been quick to defend their honor and protect their tribe.

them their choice of submitting or being killed. This was the first time he used military force.

His next objective was the conquest of Mecca. As a first step he ordered a surprise attack upon a richly laden Meccan caravan during a month of truce. His small force defeated the fighters who came to defend it. With this victory, Mohammed made himself ruler of the district; then he blockaded Mecca. In 630 A.D., A.H.8, the city opened its gates to him without a struggle. He gave amnesty to all and forbade his soldiers to do any injury or take any loot. He declared the shrine of Mecca the sanctuary of the One True God, the most holy place of Islam. He destroyed all idols, saying "Truth has come; falsehood has vanished." With this Mecca became the recognized center of Islam; from then on, all Moslems would turn toward Mecca to pray.

The surrender of Mecca assured the submission of all Arabia. Many tribes sent delegations to Medina to offer allegiance. They were required only to declare their faith in Allah, the One God, and in Mohammed, His Prophet, and to pay a tax for the poor.

Two years later, 632 A.D., Mohammed and many followers made a pilgrimage to Mecca. In what proved to be his last sermon, he proclaimed the brotherhood of all Moslems, saying: "Know ye that every Moslem is a brother unto every other Moslem. It is not legitimate for any one of you to appropriate unto himself any thing that belongs to his brother."

Shortly after his return to Medina, the Prophet fell ill with fever and died in his sixty-second year. His last words were: "God forgive me, have compassion on me, and receive me into the blessed companionship on high." Abu Bekr, who was with him, stooped and kissed his face and said, "Sweet you were in life and sweet in death, dearer than father or mother to me."

Mohammed had accomplished his mission in the short span of twenty years. He had freed the Arabs from idolatry and given them a national religion. He had made one hundred tribes of diverse customs with ancient feuds conscious of their common life and united them into the Arab nation. He left behind him dreams of a world-empire of Allah and an army trained to carry out these dreams. He had become the ideal which every devout Moslem seeks to imitate. He had spoken words which, recorded as the Koran, became the first book written in the Arabic language and which is still the masterpiece of Arabic prose. He declared himself "the seal"—the last of the prophets of God; and Moslems, throughout the centuries, have believed him.

Every follower of Mohammed turns toward Mecca to pray.

THE KORAN: THE SACRED BOOK OF ISLAM

MOHAMMED made no plans to have his words preserved except in the memory of his people, but after his death Abu Bekr collected his sayings "from palm-leaves, skins, blade-bones, and the hearts of men." This was the Koran, the sacred book of Islam. Moslems believe that it contains the very words spoken by Allah to Mohammed.

The scriptures of other religions come from various sources and authors and have been collected over long periods of time. The Koran—that which is recited—is the pronouncement of one man and was given to his hearers within a period of twenty years.

So far as is known the Koran was the first Arabic literary product put into writing. In it the Arabic language took definite form. With the spread of Islam the language of the Koran became the language of schools and courts from India to Spain. Today it is the living language of fifty million people and the sacred language of the entire Moslem world. Although the people of Islam belong to many different races and live in many countries the Koran is always read and prayers are said in Arabic. The faithful in every land greet one another with "Salam un'alaykum"—Peace be with you. Arab children learn to read from the Koran and it is the basis for instruction in law, ethics, philosophy, and religion.

The Koran consists of one hundred fourteen suras—chapters. The whole is somewhat shorter than the New Testament. Mohammed made large use of Biblical material, for he wanted to make his people conscious of their share in that ancient history.

Moslems believe that God himself wrote a book before the creation of the world. This they call the Mother Book. Revelations of this book are found in the Law of Moses, the Gospel of Jesus, and the Koran of Mohammed. The one given to Mohammed is the final authority.

Orthodox Moslems think that the Koran can be understood correctly only in Arabic, the language in which Allah spoke to Mohammed. In spite of that, there are now translations into about forty languages.

Arabic speaking children learn to read from the Koran and are early taught the Five Pillars of their faith. Even the shifting sands can be used to teach the unchanging truths of Mohammed.

THE FIVE PILLARS OF ISLAM

ISLAM IS often likened to a temple resting upon five pillars—faith, prayer, fasting, almsgiving, and the pilgrimage to Mecca.

FAITH

On every occasion of life the Moslem repeats the simple creed: "I bear witness that there is no God but Allah and that Mohammed is the Prophet of Allah." He who makes this profession of faith is a Moslem.

The idea of One God was not new when Mohammed gave it to the Moslems. Jews and Christians had worshiped one God, but the Jew had made his God primarily the God of his own people; the Christian talked about a Son of God, equal to God Himself. This seemed to Mohammed sacrilege. "They say, 'The Merciful has taken to Himself a son.' This is a monstrous thing! The heavens well-nigh burst asunder thereat, and the earth is riven! that they attribute unto the Merciful a son! There is none in the heavens or the earth but comes before the Merciful as a servant."

> "God the Eternal!
> He is God alone!
> He begets not and is not begotten!
> Nor is there like unto Him any one!"

This simple thought Mohammed presented to his people with the force of immediate revelation. The only true God had spoken to him; He had commanded that no other gods should be associated with Him; that no idol should be made, no image of any thing in heaven above or earth beneath. This idea was startlingly new to those accustomed to tribal gods and spirits everywhere, but Mohammed's conviction was so intense, his speech so compelling, that the Arabs believed him, except those whose livelihood depended upon the worship of the old gods.

Later philosophers would attempt to answer all the difficult questions about the nature of such a supreme being, but for the masses of Moslems throughout the centuries, it has been enough to know that "He is God alone" and that "He is merciful and compassionate." Every sura but one in the

Koran begins with the words, "In the name of Allah, the Compassionate, the Merciful." He knows every believer before his birth, is closer to him "than his jugular vein," watches over all his doings. A man may turn to Him with humility but also with trust. No priest or mediator is needed, for God is indeed merciful; none could avail, for in the end each man must appear singly before his Judge.

Allah is called by many names in the Koran; most of them are qualities or titles, such as The Eternal, The Mighty, The Guardian, The Restorer. The faithful use "the ninety-nine" names in their devotions as they tell their rosaries. But even these do not exhaust Him, as a popular conumdrum suggests. "Why is the camel so independent and haughty?" The answer is, "Allah has a hundred names; man knows ninety-nine, only the camel knows the hundredth and he will never tell."

"There is no God but Allah." But there are angels and archangels whom Allah created from light and who are His servants. There are also evil spirits—the powerful Satan and the many little jinn, who were created out of fire, who tempt and annoy men. The names and many stories about these supernatural beings had come from Persia.

"I bear witness that Mohammed is the Prophet of God." So every faithful Moslem declares. Yet Moslems do not think that Mohammed is the only Prophet. They honor also Adam, the Chosen of God; Noah, the Preacher of God; Abraham, the Friend of God; Moses, the Converser with God; Jesus, the Spirit of God; and Mohammed, the Prophet of God. The Moslem believes that Mohammed is the "seal" of the prophets and that after him there will be no other. He calls attention to the fact that, in the thirteen centuries since Mohammed, no prophet has arisen who has preached a universal message and secured a large following.

Yet neither Mohammed nor his followers have claimed that he is superhuman. Humbly he said, "Am I more than a mortal messenger?" and again, "Praise me not as Jesus is praised. I am liable to err as other men. I too need forgiveness." His disciples never asked signs of his authority; when his enemies did, he told them that the Koran itself was the miracle; there would be no other.

He disclaimed book-learning, but this does not necessarily mean that he could not read or write. He wished to make clear that his revelations came to him from above, directly from the "Mother Book" in heaven, not second-hand, from the study of other books.

Mohammed had unshaken confidence that he had supreme authority on earth. Submission to God meant submission to his Prophet. But his authority came from God. When a tribal chief addressed him as "Our Prince," Mohammed replied, "No, Allah is Our Prince."

The Moslem has enthusiastic faith that Allah is in absolute control; everything happens by His decree. There are tablets in heaven, written before the creation, which record all future happenings. Man can only submit and accept what Allah sends. There is no need to worry. "Nothing will afflict us save what Allah has ordained for us."

The Sky-tree of Persia, it is said, has on it a leaf for every person; on a certain night it sheds the leaves of those who are to die during the year ahead. That the hour of death is fixed for every one is a definite part of the Moslems' belief; so they face the uncertainties and sorrows of life with resignation. "It is the will of Allah" friends say to the relatives of one who has died, and they reply, "I am content with His decree." This fatalism brings comfort in sorrow, lessens the bitterness of resentment against a wrong, tends to the contentment so general among Moslems. Yet Moslems are urged to work and fight for their religion and are held responsible for their acts. How to reconcile human responsibility and freedom with absolute control by Allah is one of the problems with which philosophers and theologians have struggled.

*Paradise is "the Garden" with
cool streams, shading trees.*

The Koran teaches that two angels accompany each man through life
and record all that he does; they visit him in his grave and inquire con-
cerning his belief; if he professes his faith, "There is no God but Allah
and Mohammed is His Prophet," he is allowed to rest in peace until the
Final Resurrection.

When the Day of Judgment comes, heaven and earth will quake and be
torn asunder, mountains will fall, the sun will be darkened, the dead will rise,
and then "When Hell shall be ablaze and when Paradise shall be brought
nigh, the soul shall know what it has produced." The Koran gives vivid
pictures of the convulsions of nature and of the experiences of individual
souls, which are similar to Persian, Jewish, and Christian descriptions. Hell
is "the Fire," from which there is no escape; Paradise is "the Garden" with
cool streams and welcome shade, fresh fruits, rest, companions, and servants
—all that a desert-dweller most desires. Into this Paradise each man must
earn his way.

Later tradition embellished the words of Mohammed with oriental abun-
dance of horrors and delights, but the more sober and devout Moslem does
not think of material rewards and punishments.

"O God, if I worship Thee in fear of Hell,
Burn me in Hell.
If I worship Thee in hope of Paradise,
Exclude me from Paradise.
But if I worship Thee for Thine Own Sake,
Withhold not from me Thine everlasting beauty."

PRAYER

MOHAMMED wished to make Allah the foremost reality in the lives of his followers, so he taught them to pray five times a day. This constant practice of prayer keeps Moslems conscious, however dimly, of the presence of God. It has made Islam a sturdy faith and a closely knit fellowship.

Prayer may be offered wherever the worshiper is when the hour overtakes him. In all the broad expanse of earth there is no place where God is not. But the space in which a man prays must be marked off as a sacred spot; a piece of plain cloth or a small rug serves this purpose. A prayer rug is woven with a point in the pattern at one end; the rug is placed with this point toward Mecca, whether it is north, south, east, or west of the man who prays.

Most Moslem men go for at least one of the prayers of the day to the mosque—masjid, a place to prostrate one's self. Though many gather, the worship is usually individual. Each man removes his shoes as he enters the holy place, spreads his mat, and is ready for prayer.

Standing, he repeats "Allahu akbar!"—God is great! then recites the Fatihah, the first sura of the Koran:

"In the name of Allah, the Compassionate, the Merciful.
Praise be to God, Lord of the worlds, King of the Judgment Day.
Thee only do we worship; to Thee we cry for help.
Guide us on the straight path,
The path of those to whom Thou hast been gracious,
Not of those with whom Thou art angry nor of those who go astray."

Then he bends, kneels, prostrates himself, according to the fixed ritual, reciting prescribed quotations from the Koran. As the ritual is repeated by every Moslem from two to four times at each of the five daily prayers, the Fatihah is probably used oftener than any other prayer of any religion.

At this tank in the Great Mosque of Delhi, worshipers perform ablutions, washing the face, hands, arms to the elbow, feet, and ankles, for Mohammed said, "Purity is half of faith." There is no distinction of race, color, or social status, and this outward washing is a symbol of the cleansing power of prayer.

Five times a day—at dawn, at noon, in the mid-afternoon, at sunset, and at nightfall—the call to prayer rings out in Moslem lands. Mohammed did not wish to use the trumpet to summon worshipers, as the Jews did, nor the wooden clapper used instead of a bell by early Christians; so he chose the human voice. The crier—muezzin faces each of the four directions in turn, and—calls out in words first used by Mohammed himself: "Allah is great! I bear witness that there is no God but Allah. I bear witness that Mohammed is his Prophet. Come to prayer. Come to salvation. Allah is great! There is no God but Allah!" And the worshipers answer the call.

[41]

"The earth is a mosque for you. Therefore, wherever the time of prayer reaches you, there pray."

In the desert, where there is no water for ablutions, clean sand may be used, for "Allah desires for you what is easy, not what is hard."

Friday is the sacred day of public prayer. Every mosque has an "Imam," an officer whose duty and privilege it is to lead the worship. He stands in front of the congregation, facing toward Mecca as all do. Whether there are ten or ten thousand, the worshipers bow, kneel, prostrate themselves, and rise with perfect rhythm and smoothness as when a field of grain bends and rises before the wind. There are no reserved places in a mosque; the poorest kneels next to the richest—to affirm the brotherhood of all Moslems.

A sermon follows the Friday noon prayer-service. Attendance at this service is required of all men and boys. Mohammed did not forbid women to go to the mosque, but advised that it was better if they prayed at home.

The sanctuary of the mosque is sacred to prayer. The devout may enter at any hour to pray or to sit in some corner and recite, perhaps from memory, perhaps from the written page of a Koran chained to a low desk, words long familiar but bringing ever fresh assurance and challenge. Mohammed frowned upon any other use of the sanctuary. He is reported to have said: "Do not sit in a circle and talk before prayer."

According to tradition, Mohammed said: "The earth is a mosque for thee; therefore wherever the time of prayer reaches thee, there pray."

For many, the prayer is no more than a religious duty, suitably performed; for many, it is an oft-repeated renewal of submission to God; to some, it is the expression of continuous living with God, an experience very real to many Orientals.

Individuals may enter a mosque at any hour to pray. They face the prayer niche, which is so placed that they pray toward Mecca. The niche is often elaborately decorated. Next to it is the high pulpit, with a stairway whose sides are of carved wood or fine mosaics of tile or marble, stone or wood. These Egyptians are worshiping in a Cairo mosque.

Mosques are brightly lighted to commemorate Mohammed's illumination on the Night of Power in the month of Ramadan.

RAMADAN: THE MONTH OF FASTING

Mohammed called upon his followers to fast, following the example of devout Jews and Christians whom he knew. He set aside the month of Ramadan for this purpose, because at its end comes the "Night of Power," the night in which he received his first revelation. There are other days when the most faithful fast, but Ramadan is the only fast which is commanded for all.

Fasting is observed every day of that month from sunrise to sunset, beginning as soon as "you can discern a white thread from a black one." One may take neither food nor drink nor may he smoke. Each Moslem should recite or hear the entire Koran during the month. To make this easier it is divided into portions for each day. During Ramadan the faithful spend as much time as possible in the mosque, to "glorify God for His goodness and be grateful." Lanterns are hung from the tops of minarets and the lamps inside the mosques are lighted for the evening prayer. A brilliant illumination of the chief mosques commemorates Mohammed's illumination on the Night of Power.

A cannon or gun announces both the rising and the setting sun. One fired two hours before sunrise gives warning that it is time to prepare the early morning meal. At sunset the well-to-do often give large parties, remembering with gratitude that "God would make the fast an ease, not a difficulty."

Ramadan is the ninth month of the Moslem year, which follows a lunar calendar. It is a shifting month, coming sometimes in the winter, sometimes in the summer. The month begins when the new moon is first seen and ends with the appearance of the following new moon. When the days are short and cool, the fast is no great hardship, for the meal of dawn is made generous and the break of fast at sunset is the more welcome because of the long wait. But when the sun pours down hot and relentless through a long summer day and the whole body is parched with thirst, the self-discipline involved in not taking even a drink of water is a genuine act of devotion.

Moslems believe that Ramadan trains in self discipline. It quiets the spirit and subdues the passions; it gives a sense of unity with all Moslems everywhere; according to the Koran, it atones for all the sins of the year.

But all the values of fasting may be cancelled by lack of sincerity. "If a keeper of the fast does not abandon lying, God does not care about his leaving off eating and drinking." "There are many keepers of fasts who gain nothing except thirst, and there are many risers up at night to pray who gain nothing but wakefulness."

ALMSGIVING

In most Moslem countries, there is no organized charity to provide for the poor. The aged and the orphan, the needy and the stranger are dependent upon private generosity. A man should give one tenth of his income in alms and for the support of schools and mosques.

Mohammed knew what it meant to be an orphan and poor, to have been given a home. He to whom God has been bountiful has a debt to pay. Gabriel in one of the revelations said:

"Did He not find thee an orphan and give thee shelter?
And find thee erring and guide thee?
Wherefore as for the orphan, oppress him not:
And as for the beggar, drive him not away
But declare the goodness of the Lord."

Many a mosque in Palestine has a fig tree in the court yard, whose fruit is for the needy. The poor have the same rights as the birds; they may eat but not carry away.

Beggars by the roadside ask for alms in the name of Allah. Even those who do not give to them, answer with courtesy, praying that Allah may supply every need.

Most gracious of all the commands of the Koran are those in behalf of orphans, of slaves, of the needy, of wayfarers.

"Make not your alms vain by taunts and annoyance, like him who expends what he has for the sake of appearances before men and believes not in God and the Last Day."

"You cannot attain to righteousness until you expend in alms of what you love. What you expend God knows."

"The likeness of those who expend their wealth in God's way is as grain that grows to seven ears, in every ear a hundred grains; for God will multiply unto whom He pleases."

One of the early heads of the Moslem community wrote: "Prayer carries us half-way to God; fasting brings us to the door of His palaces; almsgiving procures for us admission."

THE PILGRIMAGE TO MECCA: THE HAJJ

FROM EARLIEST TIMES Mecca had been the center for Arab pilgrimages and markets. Mohammed, wisely deciding to preserve as much as possible of the traditional customs of his people, commanded his followers to make a pilgrimage to Mecca every year. Now once in a lifetime suffices. Most pilgrims visit Mecca at the time of the Great Festival in the twelfth month.

The Great Mosque which surrounds the Ka'aba, was built in the early Moslem centuries and has a court large enough to receive thirty-five thousand worshipers at a time. Mohammed declared the territory around the Ka'aba sacred and forbidden to any except believers, a restriction still rigidly enforced.

Mohammed gave his new religion antiquity and authority by associating Abraham with Mecca—Abraham, the Friend of God, who had established the pure religion of submission to the One God, which Mohammed was called to re-establish. He declared that the spring of Mecca was the well where Hagar found water for her son Ishmael, when they were famishing in the desert; the oasis it created was the place which Abraham loved to visit when he wearied of the less free life of Palestine; Abraham and Ishmael together built the Ka'aba.

Every year pilgrim caravans cross the deserts, plains and mountains of central Africa. Other caravans travel along the coastlands of the Mediterranean, and still others follow ancient trade routes from southern Arabia. Piles of loose stones along the trails mark the burial places of those who do not survive to complete the journey. Pilgrims from the Balkans, Turkey and Syria can now journey by rail as far as Medina. From Persia, India, Malaya and China they come by sea. Could the Indian Ocean tell its secrets, there would be stories of many who had been swept overboard by surging waves or who had died from hunger, exposure and disease.

Unseaworthy ships sometimes sink with all aboard, unable to carry longer their too heavy human cargo through the rough seas of a typhoon. There is no lament for the dead, for he who dies on pilgrimage is a martyr for his faith and is received into Paradise without questioning.

The distress of being penned for weeks like cattle on decks too crowded for movement, the perils of the desert treks—hunger, thirst, exhaustion, wild beasts and bandits—are all forgotten when the pilgrim reaches the Holy City, goal of a life-time of sacrifice and saving.

As a pilgrim approaches the sacred territory he puts on two pieces of white cotton cloth. Then with a prayer he runs to the shrine, shouting continuously, "Labbaika!"—Here I come! or At Thy Service!—no one knows the exact meaning of the ancient phrase. He circles the Ka'aba seven times, stopping each time to touch or kiss the sacred black stone—a rite common in the worship of stones.

On the first afternoon, the pilgrims, all dressed alike in the simple garb, go to a hill twelve miles from Mecca and make camp. The slope of the hill and the plain are covered with coffee-houses and stalls as at the old Arab fairs. The time is spent in prayers and diversions. On the third day, the Day of Sacrifice, they run toward Mecca. Midway they stop and each pilgrim sacrifices an animal. Part of the flesh is used for a communal meal; the rest is given to the poor. With this the Hajj is over.

The pilgrim lays aside his sacred garment and puts on his everyday clothes. The Ka'aba too, whose usual mantle of black brocade embroidered in gold has been replaced by white, is dressed again in a new black robe made each year in Cairo and brought to Mecca in a splendid procession.

More than any other institution, the Hajj shows Mohammed's statesmanship. The scattered Arab tribes had one thing in common—the pilgrimage, and at Mecca, tribal hostilities, differences of race, language, country, class are forgotten.

For the Moslem of today, Mecca has thirteen centuries of associations. Here the founder of the faith spent his childhood and received his revelations; here the struggle between the new faith and old superstitions was fought out; here the new religion won its first great triumph; and to this place thousands of pilgrims have come and countless millions have turned their faces five times a day as they worship Allah, the Great, the Merciful, to whom no other can be compared.

Every child has seen the returning Hajji, wearing the green turban which proves he has been in Mecca, and has seen the good luck sign painted over his door. He has heard his tales of adventure and has kept the persistent dream of the time when he too may join the pilgrim throng. After he has made the journey, when he turns toward Mecca to pray, he sees once more the sacred Ka'aba and the vast fellowship of which he knows himself a part. More than anything else, the Hajj binds into one the whole Moslem community.

In the time of Mohammed, raids and wars provided the romance and adventure of the nomads' life. Loot was an important part of their livelihood and the constant lure of fertile lands tempted them beyond the confines of the desert.

THE HOY WAR: JIHAD

Islam has been spread by a two-edged sword, fighting for Allah and for conquest. Mohammed appealed to the fighting instincts of the Arabs, calling his followers to a Holy War—Jihad, which means supreme effort. He assured them that "guarding the frontiers of Islam for one day was worth more than the whole world." He also promised rich booty. The conviction that Allah was fighting on their side grew stronger with every victory. The soldiers were fearless because they knew that "no soul will die but with the permission of Allah, death means Paradise, victory means pillage, defeat means only the chance to try again." The armies of Islam were irresistible.

Mohammed said, "It is not lawful to make war without first calling the infidels to the faith." He offered the enemy three alternatives: to accept Islam, surrendering to Allah and His Prophet; to submit politically and pay a tax without accepting the new religion—this was allowed only to "people of the Book," that is, Jews or Christians; or to fight and, if defeated, submit or be killed. "Kill the idolaters wherever you find them; take them and besiege them and lie in wait for them; but, if they repent and are steadfast in prayer and give alms, let them go their way; verily, God is forgiving and merciful." "The infidels shall not escape us; they shall not weaken God." "Fight until sedition be at an end and the religion be all of it God's."

When Islam was securely established, most Moslems considered that fighting was no longer a duty except when the religious ruler issued a "general summons" in case any of the people of Allah suffered wrong. Then all Moslems, men and women, east and west, must answer the call. Today the average Moslem believes that "war is a permanent institution until the Day of Judgment" and looks forward to the time when a new leader, sent by Allah, will lead the entire host of Islam in a world-wide Jihad. Officially this view has little support now, for Islam is wide-spread under governments which are not unfriendly. Progressive Moslems think of Jihad in a social sense, as "supreme effort" to overcome poverty and evil.

Will there—can there be again a Jihad? Conditions in the Middle East, India, and Indonesia make this an urgent question. There is no commanding ruler, no central authority to give the summons; but, if thoroughly aroused and united, Islam may again become a powerful host, defending all believers against the infidels and seeking new conquests.

THE CONQUERING HOSTS OF ISLAM

The expansion of the young Moslem state was endangered by the death of the Prophet, but three of his most loyal followers, Abu Bekr, Omar, and Ali, served in turn as successor—Caliph is the Arabic title. They held the loyalty of the Moslem Arab tribes and extended the borders of Islam through Syria and Iraq, westward to Egypt and along the African coast. They did not spread ruin in the lands they conquered, but settled colonies of Moslems in them. In this way they gradually won their subjects to the religious and social standards of Islam.

After Ali's death, the governor of Syria seized control and transferred the political center from Medina to Damascus. The chief concern of the new dynasty was not religion, but power and wealth. Its ninety years of rule were years of rapid conquest such as the world has seldom seen. Armies and settlers pushed across the Euphrates and the high plateaus of Persia, through mountain passes to the borders of India and China.

Other Arabs, the Moors, crossed from North Africa into Spain, quickly overcame resistance there, and swarmed over the Pyrenees into France. They were driven out of France by Charles Martel in 732 A.D. but they stayed in Spain for seven hundred years, writing one of the most glorious chapters in Spanish history. They rebuilt the old cities in Arabic style with strong forts, rich mosques, and graceful palaces. They revived agriculture with irrigation and terraces. Spain became one of the foremost centers of Moslem power and culture. The illustrious men in its mosques and universities made rich contributions to science, literature, and philosophy. The grace of its buildings, the beauty of its gardens, are still there.

In time Christians in northern Spain rallied and won back their part of the country, limiting the Moorish power to the small kingdom of Granada. In 1492 A.D., the year in which the New World was added to the Spanish empire, Ferdinand and Isabella succeeded in driving the last of the Moors out of Spain, but the culture they had developed persisted.

One hundred years after the death of Mohammed, the Arab race had pushed far beyond narrow desert boundaries. The faith he preached had united peoples of many tongues and races. The state he founded had become an empire, reaching from the Atlantic to the Indus.

The Alhambra, the fortress palace of Granada, which the Moors held for two hundred years after they had been driven out of the rest of Spain.

Court of the Myrtles. The most famous of all Moslem patios.

Court of Alhambra. The repeated units of geometric design are characteristic of Moorish art which reached its culminating point in the ornament of the Alhambra.

In this vast, loosely knit empire, semi-independent rulers struggled for power. One of these, a Persian, overthrew the reigning house in 762 A.D. and established another dynasty. The third era in the history of Islam began. No longer Arabs but Persians had the most influence in the Moslem world. The center of empire shifted eastward. The capital was Bagdad, the "City of Peace" of the Arabian Nights. Under Haran al-Rashid, fifth in succession, the Caliph whose name and splendor are familiar legend, Islam enjoyed a golden age, drawing richly upon the many cultures its world-conquests had brought together.

The dynasty lasted five hundred years, but the later Persian Caliphs had little real power, for this had passed to the Turks. They were nomads whose homeland was Turkestan in central Asia. They had migrated to the west, had become Moslems, and had gained great power. They carried their military campaign as far west as Asia Minor.

In the thirteenth century, Persia was caught in another mighty migration. Genghis Khan, the mighty conqueror in far distant Mongolia, had subdued China and then led his victorious armies westward. Nothing stopped him and his successors until they had conquered most of the Moslem territory. They also invaded Russia, Hungary, Austria, and Poland, spreading Moslem influence although not themselves Moslem.

When at last, satisfied with their booty, these Mongols returned home, another Turkish tribe, named Ottoman from their founder Othman, moved in. They conquered Christian Constantinople, now Istambul, and made it their capital. The crescent was the symbol of their sovereignty. This they had taken from the ancient Persians, who had used it to represent the horns of the bull-god. It signified the worship both of the bull, sacred in several early religions, and also of the moon, the chief deity of many desert tribes. The Ottoman Turks continued to be the leaders of Islam for almost five hundred years. Their Sultan-Caliphs were the most powerful influence throughout the Near and Middle East.

In World War I, Turkey sided with Germany against the Allies and lost. Their humiliating defeat caused revolution in Turkey. Kemal Ataturk, an intrepid leader, came to power. He sensed the need of reform; Turkey turned its face to the west and became a modern nation.

Now Islam has no Caliph, no central head, either political or spiritual, but this has not seriously lessened its religious power. Its three hundred million adherents are united not by external authority or formal organization, but by a common faith, common observances, the consciousness that they are all brothers, and loyalty to their Founder and Prophet. Islam is still a virile and growing religion.

One of the oldest streets in Bagdad, unchanged since the times when Caliph Haran al-Rashid walked here incognito.

This every day scene in Bokhara, Turkestan, recalls the story of Ali Baba and The Forty Thieves, one of the best known tales of the Arabian Nights.

Modern Istambul on the Bosphorus was Christian Constantinople, which the Ottoman Turks conquered in 1453. It became the intellectual center of Islam and remains the finest monument to its glory. Santa Sophia, the mosque to the right, was first built as a Christian cathedral. The Turks transformed it into a mosque. It has recently been made a national museum of both Christian and Moslem art.

Minaret of the mosque in Damascus which is second in age only to the Dome of the Rock in Jerusalem. It was built when Damascus became the political center of Islam, one hundred years after Mohammed's death.

Mongolia, from which Genghis Khan, "the scourge of God," led his hordes against the West in the 13th century. Today it is disputed territory between China and Russia.

Moslem Conquerors rode triumphantly through this gate in Teheran, capital of Persia (Iran). The beautiful tiles are specimens of an ancient Persian art.

The Kuyber Pass. In the whirlwind compaign of the first Moslem century, the armies of Islam pushed over difficult mountain passes to the fertile plains of northern India. The Kuyber Pass is the one now most used by travelers, trade, and soldiers.

Crusader's Vision of the Cross. By Dore'.

CRUSADES AND COUNTER CRUSADES

The most celebrated religious wars in history were the struggles between Islam and Christianity called the Crusades. One look at a map of the eastern hemisphere will show that the land of Syria and Palestine, the narrow strip between the Mediterranean Sea and the Arabian desert, is the inevitable meeting place of East and West. From the earliest days of history, conflicts have arisen there. Always racial and religious differences, competing economic and political interests have produced dangerous tensions.

In 1010 A.D. the Egyptian Caliph destroyed the buildings over the Holy Sepulchre in Jerusalem, the most sacred place in the world to Christians, the place where they believe Jesus was buried. There was an immediate call for revenge. The Catholic Pope in southern France appealed to all Christians to "enter upon the road to the Holy Sepulchre and wrest it from the wicked race." The appeal to religious emotion is always a powerful stimulus. Within a few months a hundred and fifty thousand Christians from all parts of Europe had gone east to win back the Sepulchre and to prepare the way for future pilgrims. They carried the cross on their banners and wore it as a badge; hence the name "crusaders."

Even children caught the spirit of devotion. A French shepherd lad, Stephen, certain that he had had a divine call, enlisted thousands of other boys, whom he promised to lead dry-shod across the sea; but they were kidnapped and sold in slave markets in Egypt. Another group, led by a German boy, Nicolas, suffered frightful hardships and privations, and not a single child survived to reach his goal. The Legend of the Pied Piper of Hamlin is thought to be an echo of their departure from home.

At first, the Crusaders made rapid conquest. June 7, 1099, they stood before Jerusalem. They marched barefoot around the city, blowing horns, hoping the walls would fall by a miracle similar to that of Jericho two thousand years before; but only after a long siege did the garrison surrender.

For the Moslems whose capital at this time was Bagdad, far removed from the scene cf action, the struggles in Syria were nothing worse than annoyances. However, after fifty years, they began a series of counter crusades. The Caliph, Saladin, unified Islam by proclaiming Jihad, summoning the faithful to "set free the mosque in Jerusalem to which Allah once led Mohammed." He destroyed the political power the Crusaders had gained. He allowed Christians to stay in the land if they accepted his sovereignty, for this was what Mohammed had ordered for treatment of "people of the Book." Europe answered with another Crusade, in which the rulers of England, Germany, and France all took the cross. After three years the Moslem forces were victorious. Saladin entered and "purified" Jerusalem. However, he allowed small bands of Crusaders to continue to visit the Holy Sepulchre and the Christian forces retained some of the coastal lands of Syria.

After Saladin's death, there were other crusades and many petty wars, but they had political rather than religious significance. The end came in 1291 A.D. with the fall of the Syrian seaport, Acre, to the armies of Egypt; this had been the last stand of the Christians.

Many of the Crusaders' Castles and some of their churches survive in Syria and Palestine, mostly in ruins. In the modern population of those countries there are evidences of European blood; some family names are of French origin; some people have fair complexions, blue eyes, and light hair. The use of the French language as the international language of the East dates back to the leadership of France during these centuries.

The Crusades were of more significance for the West than for the East, for the culture of Islam was more advanced than that of Europe. The Crusades had greatly stimulated commerce. Europeans had acquired new tastes in food, clothing, and personal habits. They welcomed products from the East—muslins from Mosul, damasks from Damascus, and cotton, Arabic qutun, and new dyes, indigo, lilac, and crimson. There were new plants and crops—rice, melons, pepper, ginger, and other spices, and sugar from sugar cane; before this, molasses had been the only sweetening for European tables. Men came back wearing beards as the men of Syria still do. Cross-stitch embroidery, the characteristic decoration of women's clothes in Syria, found favor in Europe. The rosary, whose use the Moslems had learned from the Buddhists of India, was adopted in Christian ritual. Stained glass windows appeared in churches, for Tyre and Sidon had early perfected the art of glass making.

The financial needs of merchants and traders led to the establishment of consular offices and a system of international banking. Europeans learned from the Moslems the systematic care of the sick. They adopted the training of carrier pigeons, the wearing of heavy mail armor, the use of armorial bearings and the rules of heraldry, and the custom of celebrating victories by illuminations and by hanging banners from windows and on walls. In these and more significant ways, contact with Islam hastened the reawakening of the West, the Renaissance.

Ruins of Crusaders' castles and churches, built during the two hundred years in which the Crusaders dominated the land, are still standing in Syria and Palestine. Kala Ta Hussan, shown above, is one of the best preserved.

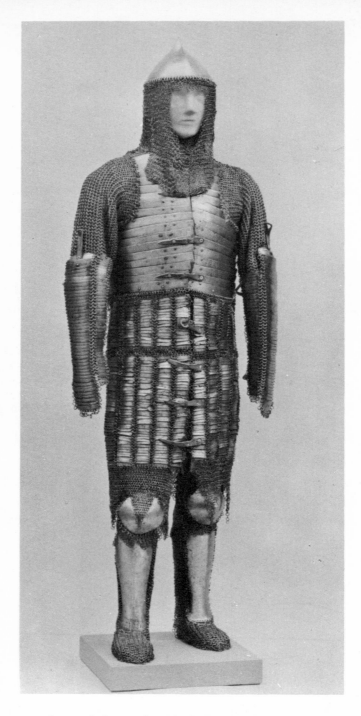

Europeans learned from the Moslems to use chain mail armor.

Polo was a Moslem game before it was known to Europe.

MOSLEM LAW

The Law, as Moslems use the word, is a broader term than law as generally understood in the West. It embraces every concern of life. Its decrees are not man's decisions, but God's decrees. The Koran is final and the interpretations and applications which the early scholars made still have binding authority. Law has been the most significant and highly developed subject of Moslem study.

Mohammed gave much attention to the regulation of the social and economic life of the Medina community. His rules have continued to give necessary training to backward peoples and have maintained community of practice and ideals among Moslems, even when there is no political unity.

There were two main divisions of the Law, one concerned with religious duties, the other with right relations to men. Religious duties were chiefly the Five Pillars. The moral teaching echoed that of Jews and Christians. Two statements may be called the Moslem version of the Golden Rule. "Offer to men what thou desirest should be offered to thee; avoid doing to men what thou dost not wish to be done to thee." "No brother has perfectly believed until he wishes for his brother what he wishes for himself." A "brother" means a fellow-believer. The entire community was to be one family, "like a compact wall whose bricks support each other." Arab social structure was founded on the welfare of the group rather than the welfare of the individual; Mohammed enlarged the group.

"Righteousness is to him who gives cheerfully of his substance; who frees the prisoner and the slave; who fulfills the covenants to which he has bound himself; who is patient in times of distress and pain and struggle." According to the Koran, forgiveness is better than revenge; peace is better than war; to kill is forbidden except in Holy War for the faith.

Mohammed did not ask his followers to give up the ordinary good things of life; "Eat what God has provided you." Yet he, like the Jews, considered certain foods not fit to eat, especially pork and animals which have been killed in certain ways. At first he did not forbid drinking the juice of the fruit in palms and grapes; this was God's gift. Later, some men came intoxicated to pray and disturbed the service; then he forbade all use of intoxicants. These laws are faithfully observed by most Moslems.

Singing and dancing were associated with low women and were to be avoided. Mohammed also forbade raffling and all gambling, saying "Satan desires to place enmity and hatred between you by wine and games of chance and to turn you from the remembrance of God and from prayer."

In the Mosque schools, young men study the Law as given in the Koran.

WOMEN

Moslem law has much to say about women and marriage. Mohammed made efforts to improve the lot of women, although he shared the universally accepted position that men are superior to women. He prohibited the common practice of killing at birth unwanted baby girls. He constantly reminded the men of the need of kindness and that "Allah is well aware of what you do."

He commanded men to marry. To one who had determined to remain single, he said: "Either you wish to be a Christian monk, in which case join them publicly; or you belong to us. In that case you must obey our custom. Our custom demands married life." He allowed as many as four wives, but monogamy is the general practice among Moslems. Yet in a society where many men were killed in wars and raids, polygamy seemed, and still does seem to many, the most satisfactory provision for the excess women.

Mohammed advised that a man see the woman before he asks for her in marriage and stated that no woman should be married without her consent. It is reported that, when asked how she should give consent, his reply was, "Her silence is her consent." But eastern etiquette seldom allows young men and women to see each other unless they have grown up together in a small town.

A girl does everything she can to get a good husband. She uses charms and drinks potions and visits the shrine of any nearby saint. Then, having done all she can, she accepts the choice of her parents of Kismet, her fate, the will of Allah. To be a wife and mother is her appointed lot.

Marriage is a civil contract between the two fathers. The religious ceremony and the social festivities vary with the customs of the country.

Moslem women accept as unquestioningly as do the men the idea that a wife is her husband's property—"tillage" is the word in the Koran—which he has the right and duty to control. He may beat an unruly wife, but if she submits, he must not turn against her; it is better to have patience. God is forgiving and "knows that man was created weak."

Moslem women have property rights. They share in inheritances and no one can take a woman's estate against her will. If she is divorced, her husband may not take her dowry from her; if she is widowed, she retains it and is free to marry again.

Moslem husband with his four wives. The one who has a son ranks first. Mohammed allowed as many as four wives if a man could make adequate provision for them and treat them without partiality, but he warned, "if you fear that you will not act justly between them, marry only one." The practice of polygamy has not been as general as is commonly thought, first because there are not enough women for every man to have four wives and also because most men cannot afford so many. Monogamy is the general rule.

In case of ill treatment, a woman may appeal to the men of her own family. Representatives of each family may mediate when there is danger of a break between husband and wife. However, divorce is easy; it requires only the word of the husband; even the wife may demand it under certain conditions. One curious provision indicates how impulsive divorce often is. A man may not divorce the same wife more than twice and then take her back again; if he divorces her the third time, she must marry another man and be divorced by him before her first husband can have her again. If she prefers to stay with her second husband, she cannot be forced to leave him.

There is no command in the Koran that women must be secluded and veiled. The practice runs counter to Arab custom, but tradition carries it back to restrictions Mohammed placed upon his later wives. Among the people of the desert and the open country, women cover their faces only when they see strange men approaching; but in towns they do not go out uncovered. The men are very jealous for the reputation of their women and the women themselves would be embarrassed by the gaze of strangers. In cities and among the more prosperous even in small towns, the women's apartments are separate from those of the men and are entered only by husbands and sons under special arrangements. Women leave their own apartments seldom and then are covered from head to foot.

Mohammed himself took no other wife as long as his beloved Khadijah lived, and she enjoyed great freedom. Since he has become the model for his followers, it might have made life different for women of the East if he had never had another wife. After her death and his move to Medina, he married many women, not limiting himself to four. There were various motives, some personal, some political, and some humanitarian—to provide a home for a woman otherwise unprotected. Revelations from God authorized each marriage. "O thou Prophet, we make lawful to thee thy wives, a special privilege for thee above other believers."

Women who believe share in the promise of Paradise. They are expected to observe the daily prayers in their homes. Some mosques have secluded balconies for them. Today progressive men and women are trying to break through the barriers which separate them; some women are serving their communities outside their homes; but it takes courage to overstep the restrictions established by centuries of usage.

The Moslem tradition has never regarded a woman as a person in her own right; she should always be content to achieve through others. This is the quality the Oriental loves most in a wife.

*Latticed screens enclose the balconies of the Harem—the women's apartments,
so Moslem women may see without being seen.*

CHILDREN

Moslems consider the choice of a child's name very important as it may influence the whole life. Mohammed is the name most often given to boys and Fatima to girls. The fact that many illustrious men have borne the name of Mohammed makes Moslem history confusing.

Arabs as well as Jews practice the rite of circumcision. The ceremony comes most often between the seventh and the fifteenth years. It marks the passage from childhood to manhood; from then on the boy must observe the five daily prayers.

"Watch the grown-ups and do as they do" is the basic maxim in training children. The father shows the boys, the mother the girls, and very early they share in the activities of the home. The village boy goes with his father to the evening gatherings of the men, hears the stories of the past, the gossip of the town, and perhaps some discussion of larger interests. A town boy may learn some craft or trade as apprentice to a master-workman. Both are trained in good manners.

As soon as the child can talk, he learns the words with which the Koran begins: "In the name of Allah, the Compassionate, the Merciful" and the simple but basic creed: "There is no God but Allah." Almost every mosque has a small school, held on the roof or in the corridors, where the boys and sometimes the girls may learn to read and write the Koran. The youngest pupils do not attempt to write the name of Allah, lest they make a mistake, for it would never do to erase or scratch that holy word. The student memorizes much of the Koran and learns to intone it with the proper rhythm. His goal is to learn it all by heart; if he achieves this, the family and village have a celebration to honor both the boy and his teacher.

Language is a problem, for the native languages of Moslems include the most varied tongues and the spoken Arabic today is as different from the literary as Italian is from Latin. Yet every child must learn the Koran in the classic Arabic, even if he does not understand a word.

The pupil may be taught the elements of grammar and a little arithmetic, but the important thing is that he learn the teachings of his religion.

From early days there have been Moslem universities, the most famous being the University of al-Azhar in Cairo, Egypt. For almost a thousand years classes have gathered in the cloisters and halls of the mosque to study the Koran. Students come from all parts of the Moslem world. They are supported by scholarships and gifts from those who feel the obligation to pass on their religious heritage without expense to those who do not have resources.

*In the mild climate of many Moslem countries, classes meet out of doors.
Government schools now give instruction which is designed to help boys earn
a living.*

In front of the Great Mosque of Delhi, Moslems celebrate the Lesser Festival, which breaks a month of fasting. The children are enjoying a wooden Ferris wheel, turned by hand.

FESTIVALS

Moslems share the age-old and well nigh universal custom of celebrating the spring equinox, when lambs are born into the flocks, when the first flowers appear on the earth, when birds return after the winter and begin to build their nests and sing their songs of love. In Persia especially this is the gayest occasion of the year; everyone has new clothes and special food, and friends call upon friends and bring or send gifts.

Two distinctive Moslem festivals, prescribed by the Prophet, are observed throughout all Islam: the Great Festival—the Feast of Sacrifice, and the Lesser Festival—the Feast of Breaking the Fast.

The Great Festival is held upon the Day of Sacrifice, the last day of the Hajj in Mecca. This gives every Moslem a share in that celebration. The people assemble in an open place outside the city for special morning prayers and a sermon; then they return to their homes. The head of each family takes the dedicated animal—a sheep, goat, cow, or camel, and turns its head toward Mecca and slays it as he repeats suitable prayers. One third of the flesh is given to the poor, one third to relatives, and one third is used for the family feasting, which lasts for three days. This sacrifice commemorates the willingness of Abraham to offer up his beloved son Ishmael, from whom the Arabs trace their descent.

The Lesser Festival marks the end of the fast of Ramadan. Prayers and almsgiving then make certain the rewards promised for the hardships of the fast. The three day celebration begins with morning worship, out in the open when the weather permits. There are special prayers for health, good crops, preservation from all misfortune, and the forgiveness of sins. Festivities follow. This is the time for making up quarrels and for expressions of good will. Generous alms are given to the needy and people care for the tombs of their dead.

The anniversary of Mohammed's birth is a gay festival. The date has been fixed as April 20, 571 A.D. Processions, fireworks, and the booming of cannon are part of the celebration. Cantatas of the birth and life of the Prophet are sung by professional musicians at this time as well as at weddings and other occasions of rejoicing.

MOSLEM CULTURE

When the conquering generals came back to Damascus and Bagdad, men of royal birth and men of learning were among their captives; riches of art and literature among their loot. The rulers used their prisoners as teachers, advisors, physicians. The Arabs were quick to learn; they developed a new culture to which Persia and India, Greece and Rome contributed. The dark ages of Europe were not dark in Moslem lands. By the eighth century one of the most significant movements of human thought was in full swing.

In the middle of the ninth century, the ruling Caliph established in Bagdad the "House of Wisdom" as an academy for scholars. Only a few of these scholars were of Arab blood, but whoever spoke and wrote Arabic was counted an Arab. Translators worked on priceless Greek manuscripts. The Arabs did not know Greek, so Jewish scholars translated the Greek into their language, Aramaic, and Christians translated it into Syriac and from these it was translated into Arabic. In its search for knowledge, Islam knew no barriers of time, country, tongue, or even religion. Mohammed had said: "Seek learning though it be in China."

There was need of learning. Scholars made a scientific study of their grammar and formulated rules so that they could teach new converts who did not know Arabic. Preachers must learn the art of public speaking, so that their sermons on Friday would give clear ideas of the faith to those newly won to it. The Koran must be studied by jurists and religious teachers if a vast empire was to be governed by the laws of Islam. Al-Bukhari gathered and sifted thousands of traditions and made the first established collection of the best authenticated ones—a work for which he prepared himself by ablutions and prayer. Pilgrims to Mecca, coming now from far-distant lands, needed guide books for the journey and, in turn, contributed to the knowledge of geography. The Moslem love of globe-trotting is suggested by the title of a famous geography: "The Recreation of Him Who Yearns to Traverse the Lands." Schools and libraries were established in connection with many mosques; all boys were encouraged to learn to read and even girls were allowed to attend classes. In Cordova and Granada as well as in Bagdad, scholars of all nationalities were bringing together the learning of the world.

*The Arabs were the first people to carry on international trade on a grand
scale. From earliest days their "ships of the desert" had transported the
wealth of the world they knew. When they advanced in waves of conquest
they blazed trails which later railroads, motor traffic, and airplanes were
to follow. They sailed from the Persian Gulf to the east coast of Africa and
Madagascar and to the harbors of India, the East Indies, and remote China.
They charted the unknown seas. They brought back not only goods for sale
but also the priceless gifts of many cultures.*

*The art of cultivating the silkworm and making silk came from China over
"the great silk way" and became one of the flourishing industries of Syria,
Spain, Italy and France.*

An ancient sun dial that marked the month and the day as well as the hour.

The exact precision of the Arabic language and the Arabs' love of order-liness and clarity of thought fitted them for the study of mathematics. The scientific approach to trigonometry, analytical geometry, and algebra is largely the work of Arabs, as the very name algebra—from al-jebr, binding together—suggests. They brought from India a system of numerals which we use and call Arabic. Every western schoolboy can thank the Arabs that he does not have to do his sums with the cumbersome system of letters called Roman numerals. They also introduced the use of the cipher, zero—"little circles to keep the rows straight." Without this simplification from the old way of reckoning on the abacus, mathematical progress would have been difficult.

In science too the Moslems were undisputed masters. Often their conclu-sions were significant and bold. It was startling when a physician declared that the epidemic which was ravaging the country was not an act of Allah to be accepted with submission, but was the result of infection which should be avoided; he said experience, investigation, the evidence of the senses, and trustworthy reports all established the fact of contagion.

According to the tradition, Mohammed had said, "Science is two-fold, that which relates to religion and that which relates to the body." Medicine was one of the first concerns of Moslems. The early Arabs had known only magic and the use of a few herbs; but contact with Greek and Persian science led to research and practice. Schools in Bagdad trained physicians, who were required to pass examinations before they could practice. Hospitals were established and traveling physicians and clinics carried help to outlying districts and gave attention to public health. There developed an interest in chemistry, especially drugs.

Chemistry is the scientific development of alchemy. The Arabic name—al-kimiya—goes back to an ancient Egyptian word for black, indicating that the art was used in black magic. Many chemical substances have Arabic names—alcohol, alkali, elixir, syrup, alembic. The word soda has an inter-esting history; it comes from the verb "to split apart" and first meant a headache, then a headache remedy, and finally a remedy for the indigestion which sometimes caused the headache.

Astronomy had its beginning in astrology, the belief that the stars influ-ence all human fortune. Desert dwellers have always studied the heavens. Most of the names of stars in European languages have come from the Arabic, as well as such terms as zenith and nadir. The House of Wisdom in Bagdad included an observatory, which contained quadrants and other instruments for measuring celestial movements. Its influence extended to other Moslem countries. An astronomer in Cairo for the first time recorded solar eclipses with scientific accuracy. Scholars carried on careful studies to determine the circumference of the earth in case it was round, long before the fact had been established. Columbus learned their theory that the earth was round; without this the New World might not have been discovered.

Chess was an ancient game in India; one Moslem ruler played it on a great court marked off in a hundred squares with slave girls as his pawns.

Spanish gardens with terraces and irrigating canals, with oranges, pomegranates, and apricots, with shade trees and flowers, are an enduring monument to the knowledge of horticulture of the Moslem conquerors.

Many objects in use in the West show by their names that they had their origin in Moslem lands. Grenadine was first woven in Granada. Taffeta was a Persian silk called taftah. Attab, a certain section of Bagdad, called the striped and watered silk which was their specialty attabi; in time people in Europe began to call their striped cats tabby. When the Crusaders took home newly discovered sweets, they called them by their Arabic names—sukkar, sugar, and quandah, candy.

The highest Islamic culture was attained in the tenth century; since then there has been little advance. The empire was vast and poorly united; the jealousies of princes led to division into many petty kingdoms; the rulers were rich, weak, and oppressive. When sturdy Mongols came to conquer, the empire was already crumbling. Still later, the fierce Turks put an end to freedom of thought by their reactionary and rigid discipline.

So the shadows fell over the Moslem world, but not before Islam had given her legacy to Europe. From China the secret of making paper had been brought to Bagdad as early as the eighth century; this knowledge, passed on to Europe, made it possible to provide books for the masses, not merely for the rich and the scholars. The romantic Arabic literature with its color and rich imagery, its appeal to the imagination and the emotions and its romantic spirit and new forms of meter and rhyme, inspired the songs of troubadours that presently appeared.

Tales of travelers, as well as the tales of romance which they had gathered from many lands, were told and retold throughout Europe and grew in the telling. Such were the stories of Sindbad the Sailor. "The Arabian Nights" has been published in all the languages of western Europe. Their spirit of romance and adventure may have inspired such works as "Robinson Crusoe."

Europe was emerging from her darkness, thanks in large measure to the Moslems, who had kept the lights of learning bright in Spain and in the East.

*Chess was an ancient game in India. A Persian poet tells how it was intro-
duced into his country. An Indian Rajah sent a set to the Persian Shah, saying
that he would no longer pay tribute unless the Persians could work out the
moves of the game. The Shah appealed to his counselors. This Persian
miniature shows one of them explaining his solution.*

*Moslems found the game good training in military manoeuvers. Their chess-
men were chariots, elephants, horsemen, infantry—the four branches of the
army. Later simplified forms replaced the more realistic figures, partly
because of Mohammed's prohibition of making "any likeness of any living
thing."*

MUSIC

A negro named Sa'id, who traveled widely, translated the songs of other countries into Arabic, and first worked out the system which became classic for Arabic music.

Singing has always been the most common and most loved form of music, partly no doubt because of the Arabs' fondness for poetry. Most often simple instruments accompany it. Moslems early studied theories of sound and music, and the rhythmic measuring of music was practiced among the Arabs long before it was known in Europe and the use of the baton goes back to the eighth century, so the modern Drum Major is all unconsciously in their debt. They knew nothing of harmony and made little use of accent, but they adorned the melody by a companion note now and again, which perhaps prepared the way for harmony, later developed in the West.

Since instrumental music was a part of pagan ways of worship, Mohammed forbade it to his followers, saying it was "the devil's muezzin, calling men to worship him."

His objections were soon ignored. Wandering minstrels, dressed in bright colors, with painted faces and hands, would beat a drum with one hand and finger a pipe with the other, shaking the little bells upon their gay caps in keeping with the rhythm. Military bands accompanied armies and shared in the celebration of victories. They had drums, kettle-drums, pipes of many sorts, cymbals, and tambourines. Making musical instruments became a fine art.

The lute was the earliest stringed instrument; it was of many shapes and sizes. Then came the guitar—qitara, the harp, and the rabab, an instrument played with a bow. Skilled players could drive away fears and depression, as the young shepherd David did for King Saul. They visited from court to court and often brought home to their patrons secrets of importance heard over the wine cups. More modest fiddlers played at weddings, traveling from village to village, as they do today using the same instruments.

Mecca and Medina became centers of music. Musicians in gala attire accompanied the pilgrimage processions to Mecca, rivaling in interest even the festivities of the Hajj itself, for the people believed that rejoicing with music and companionship was preparation for the ecstasy of the sacred celebration.

Lute players at a Persian court.

MOSLEM ART

Moslem Art includes the art of every country to which Islam spread during the many centuries of its supremacy. It includes Turkish rugs and Egyptian mosques, Syrian glass and Damascene swords; it is cross-stitch embroidery and latticed screens; it is Persian prints and Arabian textiles; it is the Alhambra and the Taj Mahal.

All the fine arts are included except painting and sculpture. These are excluded because the Moslems took seriously the command of Moses: "Thou shalt not make unto thee any graven image or any likeness of any thing that is in the heaven above or in the earth beneath or in the waters under the earth." So Moslems were limited to geometric or conventionalized designs and purely imaginary and playful representations of animals and people. Portrait painting was unknown, for according to tradition the Prophet had said: "Those most severely punished on the Day of Judgment are the portrayers."

During the long periods of security and peace that followed conquests, the Moslems were generous patrons of the arts and the legacy of their culture in a dozen countries remains to enrich the world.

The nomad Arabs had little opportunity to express themselves in art except in poetry and music. They did not have materials or tools, and could not carry about unnecessary objects. Yet in making the necessities of life they developed certain skills and techniques. Their intense love of beauty expressed itself in adornment of pots and textiles.

Perhaps the fact that they had so little art of their own made the Arabs more responsive to the treasures to which they fell heir on their world conquests. They accepted eagerly everything beautiful which did not run counter to their religion. Yet life in the desert had developed strong feelings and ideas which profoundly influenced the art of the different countries they conquered and which give character and unity to Moslem art.

The first of these feelings was a love of freedom and spaciousness. Desert life creates an aversion to anything that shuts in; its boundlessness has space for all with no sense of limits or direction. This feeling is reflected in two pronounced ways, in the favorite pattern used throughout Moslem designs —the arabesque—and in the architectural form of the mosque.

Persian.   15th Century.

The arabesque is a flowing design of lines, leaves, flowers, and sometimes birds and animals. It encircles a wall, a doorway, or a page without beginning or end, and typifies the Moslem faith in God.

The feeling of spaciousness is also reflected in the architectural design of the mosque. There are no aisles or pews. There is no sense of direction, no distinction of parts. When required for protection, a central dome over the court of a mosque closes the space which had been left open in the early mosques, yet does not give the feeling of being shut in, as would a flat roof or squared walls. A dome has no right or left, no north or south; it is a symbol of the limitless vault of heaven. The decoration of the dome increases the sense of height. Sometimes finely carved pendent stalactites, thick as a forest of trees hanging with their heads down, make it a fairyland of delicate lines and soft colors.

Another characteristic of Moslem art is a love of detail, seen most clearly in the decorative and applied arts. Every available space and surface is filled or covered with a profusion of delicate designs, as luxurious as the growth of an oasis. The basic pattern is usually geometric. The flowers, foliage, birds, beasts, and fish, often introduced, are the things which the Moslems valued most, the ordinary things upon which desert life depends. They are pictured as ministering to the needs of man.

Mohammed's teaching discouraged art efforts. He condemned personal luxury. Devout Moslems, he said, should not wear silk nor use gold and silver utensils; these are reserved for Paradise. But the desire for beauty persisted in spite of Mohammed's efforts for simplicity and austerity.

Few names of Moslem artists have been remembered, for Mohammed taught that no man was to think of himself as apart from or superior to others. So the artist subordinates himself as he makes beautiful what is given him to express and is happy to possess in common with other artists the rich legacy of his culture. He follows accepted standards and techniques. He does not put perspective into a landscape, for the way an observer looks at things does not change what they are. He is not selective in his arrangement, for all things are of equal worth. No individual feature competes for attention, for the value is in the whole. This is the expression in art of the democracy which was so important a part of the teaching of Mohammed.

Iranian animal rug. 16th Century.

Iranian bowl. 10th Century.

Mesopotamian bowl. 12th–13th Century.

Mohammed forbade artists to make realistic images and pictures in protest against current idolatry, and in keeping with the command handed down from Moses: "Thou shalt not make unto thee any graven image or any like-ness of any thing that is in the heaven above or on the earth beneath or in the waters under the earth."

Persian bowl. 12th Century.

Wall tile. Late 12th Century, Persian.

ARCHITECTURE

The nomadic Arab had no architecture. He lived in a tent, worshiped under the open sky, buried his dead in the desert sand. The primitive mosque was scarcely a building; it was simply, as its name implies, a place where men prostrated themselves.

As Arabs conquered people of higher culture, they found buildings and skilled workmen, and they used both. Some of the churches they converted into mosques; from others they took materials for new structures. Columns from several buildings might be used in the new one. If they did not match, it did not disturb a Moslem; they were parts of the whole and not to be considered individually. There were different materials available and different building traditions in different countries, but the Moslems developed their own definite architectural form.

The supreme achievement of Moslem architecture is the mosque. The uncovered central court is enclosed, often by colonnades; in the center is a tank for ablutions. On one side, usually under cover, is the prayer niche—mihrab—so placed that in kneeling, the worshiper faces toward Mecca. To the right of the mihrab stands the high pulpit.

The columns in a mosque are of varied shapes—spiral, octagonal, or grooved. The capitals and bases may be cubical, round, or bell-shaped, sometimes richly decorated. In some cases four small columns are bound into one. Low arches unite these columns and support flat stone roofs over arcades. They too have taken on various forms—the many-foil arches of Egypt, the fan arch of Spain, the horseshoe arch of Damascus, the melon-shaped arch of India, the Persian arch in which a pointed arch runs down into straight lines before reaching the supporting pillar, and the sharply pointed arch which later became so characteristic of Gothic architecture.

The dome, a characteristic form in domestic buildings long enough ago to be seen in Assyrian reliefs, was first used in a monumental way in the Dome of the Rock in Jerusalem. In the great mosques smaller domes may be raised around the high central one. The interior may show rows of small domes supported by pillars and rows of domed cells, suggesting the cloisters of Europe.

Mosque of Isfahan in Persia.

In striking contrast to the heavy dome rises the tall slender minaret, used for the call to prayer. Minarets were also sometimes erected to commemorate victories. Mohammed did not allow a victor to be honored with a monument, for fighting was a religious duty and it was Allah who gave the victory. But a victor could erect a minaret in gratitude to Allah and add an inscription with the name of the donor.

Artists and craftsmen have lavished their gifts upon the vast domes, the towering minarets, the columns and arches, the mosaics of walls and floors, the carvings in marble and wood, the friezes and inscriptions, the lamps and rugs.

The friezes may be of tile, of carved wood, of stucco, or a combination of these and other materials. The design is exuberant. The flowing arabesque is often the background for an inscription taken from the Koran. Sometimes the whole frieze is colored in gold, red, blue, and green, with no attempt to be lifelike, rather with colors so arranged as to destroy any illusion of reality, against which Moslem thought always revolts. The rhythmic repetition of pattern in the endless flowing frieze, like the intoning of a ritual, creates an atmosphere of calm.

Below the friezes, walls may be hung with rugs or other textiles or paneled in colored marbles, incrusted stucco, carved wood, or inlays of ivory, ebony, and mother-of-pearl. Floors are of mosaic, tile, or carved white marble.

Especially rich and delicate is the decoration of the pulpit and the prayer-niche. Strict conservatives frown at these because the prayer-niche is thought to resemble the apse of Christian churches and the pulpit raises the preacher above his brethren. But in most mosques the high pulpit is ascended by stairs whose sides are of carved wood or covered with fine mosaics of tile, marble, stone or wood. Often ivory, ebony, and mother-of-pearl are combined with wood. The prayer-niche is even more resplendent with its floor of finely carved white marble or tile inlay; its dome glistening with tile mosaics; its sides covered with friezes or niches, enameled or incrusted with richly colored stucco.

Continuous rows of empty niches in many a mosque recall the vases of pottery, ivory, glass, and metal which once filled them, and which are now preserved in museums. Because Moslems were forbidden to use gold and silver, they perfected and elaborated the use of bronze, brass, and copper.

Mosaic mihrab at Isfahan. Iranian, 14th Century.

They engraved patterns or raised them in relief; they inlaid gold and silver upon the coarser metals by a process which came to be called damascene because it was first known to the West from Damascus markets. Pottery reached high perfection in the ninth century when Bagdad was in the fullness of its glory.

Luster glazes, sometimes iridescent, were developed to give all the gleam of forbidden gold; favorite colors were gold, white, green, and blue. The bright blue on white was later copied by the Chinese; they used it for some of their finest chinaware. This in turn was imported into Europe, so that today the West calls "Chinese blue-and-white" what the Chinese used to label "Mohammedan blue."

In the mosques vases of crystal and glass were most often used for lamps. Large jars were decorated by cutting or etching, by patterns melted in or encrusted, or by gold or enamel designs. These were fitted with small lamps and suspended by chains, especially impressive when lighted for some holy evening service. Stained glass windows, usually in geometric designs, were also found in mosques.

Many of the finest knotted carpets known as oriental rugs, were made for mosques. Small prayer rugs are most beautiful. Sometimes the ends are filled with blue to suggest the heaven above. The design always has a point at one end to be turned toward Mecca; within the point may hang a lamp between pillars, suggesting the mihrab. Under the fostering care of the rich kings of Bagdad, rug-making reached its highest development. Persian patterns are largely leaf, bud, and flower, sometimes birds, fish, and animals, often stylized beyond recognition. The graceful and intricate designs are worked out in delicate colors in perfect harmony. Islam never succeeded in suppressing the exuberance of Persian art.

In contrast, Turkish rugs show the influence of the rigid Moslem faith and of the bold conquerors who subdued the country. Turkish rugs never introduce animal forms; floral designs are infrequent; the patterns are usually geometric, the colors bright and arranged in bold contrasts.

The most sacred of all mosques is the one at Mecca, the great court and cloisters which surround the Ka'aba. The first Mosque of the Prophet at Medina has been rebuilt several times but it still stands upon the ancient site. Within a hundred years of the death of the Prophet it was enlarged to include the burial places of Mohammed and his two close friends and successors, Abu Bekr and Omar.

Dome of the Rock.

The third most holy shrine is in Jerusalem. No spot on earth has more hallowed associations for more people. The sacred enclosure was once the court of the temple built by Solomon, the most splendid of ancient Israel's kings. Here is the holy Rock of Sacrifice, which tradition considers the place where Abraham prepared to offer up his son, where the Hebrews offered sacrifices during long centuries. Jesus taught within these temple courts; an early Christian church stood here. Here Mohammed stopped upon his memorable night flight to heaven; his footprint upon the rock can still be seen!

When Omar conquered Palestine in 638 A.D., he cleared the sacred rock of debris and probably set up a modest place of worship. It is a mistake however to call the building which now covers the rock the Mosque of Omar, as foreigners have commonly done. Fifty years passed before the glorious shrine, the Dome of the Rock, was built. Abd al-Malik, Caliph at Damascus at the time, had it erected to provide a place of pilgrimage for Syrian Moslems less remote than Mecca. It is the earliest surviving architectural monument of Islam, a structure seldom equalled in dignity and beauty.

The Pearl Mosque, built by Aurangzeb for the use of the royal family, is seen through an arch of the Hall of Private Audience in the Red Fort of Delhi.

[104]

The solid, heavy pillars, low bases and capitals, and ogee arches in the interior of the Pearl Mosque, are characteristic of Moslem architecture in India. Prayer spaces in the marble floor point toward the prayer niche.

Turkey

Jerusalem

The tall, slender minaret, is used for the call to prayer. Near the top it is encircled by a balcony, that the muezzin may face in all four directions as he repeats his call. The derivation of the word suggests a lighthouse, for the first minaret had been a beacon tower in Damascus. The early minarets were simple; square towers tapering slightly, crowned with battlements above which rose the muezzin's stage. Later builders delighted in making them lovely both in shape and decoration.

Iraq

Egypt

Egypt

CALLIGRAPHY

Beautiful handwriting is the art most highly esteemed by Moslems, for its first use was to transmit the revelation God gave to Mohammed. The Arabic script is very decorative whether in flowing lines or in the stiff angular style, stately and solemn as befits the Holy Book. The exquisitely handlettered Korans in museums and collections of art patrons all over the world testify to the zeal with which Moslems have always worked to master this supreme art. "To copy in the most perfect of forms the most perfect of books" has been their goal, and attaining it was one of the ways to secure admission to Paradise.

The Arabic alphabet is easily adapted to decorative design. Most of its twenty-eight letters are based on curves and the others on parallel lines. The best pages by master calligraphers with perfectly proportioned margins and harmonious spacing between the lines are often framed and hung upon the wall as paintings are in the western world.

Beautiful examples of calligraphy are to be found in every country where the Moslems settled but it was the Persians who valued most the various Arabic scripts and who made calligraphy a fine art. They concentrated on it for centuries, employed their best artists to create new letter forms and their finest craftsmen to adapt them as decoration for almost everything they made. Whether it was a medallion or a manuscript, a plate or a prayer rug, a doorway or a dome, there was some letter of the alphabet or some inscription from the Koran to fill the space perfectly. It was one thing however to design an alphabet that was beautiful in a book with pages a few inches wide, and quite another when the same alphabet was used on a frieze for a wall ten feet high. Enlarging the letters would reveal many flaws and suggest improvements. It was in the constant effort to perfect each letter and each part of each letter, and in the harmonious relation of each letter to the alphabet as a whole that genius triumphed. The Persians were never satisfied when they had designed two or three letters of unsurpassed beauty. All the letters must conform, all details cooperate to achieve the final pattern. An alphabet with every detail so perfected and harmonized into the whole has been compared to a Mozart melody.

*Calligraphy, though hardly recognized in Europe or America, is a supreme
art in Asia.*

Illuminated title page from Mir Khusrau of Delhi.

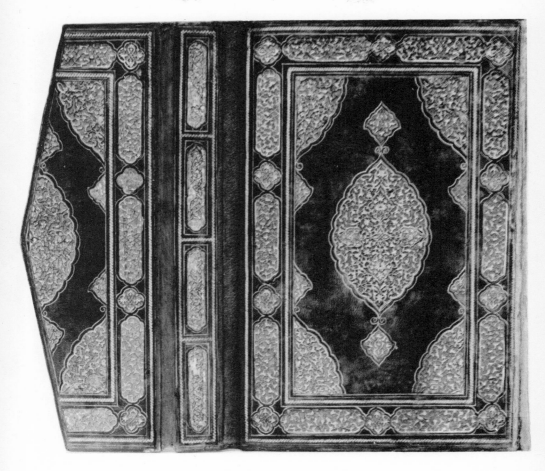

Book cover with arabesque design.

Some very old Korans have wooden covers, rich with inlays of various woods and ivory, but the most usual binding is of leather, decorated inside and out with stamping, painting, and gold. When lacquer was introduced from eastern Asia, this too was used to decorate the bindings.

For the chief festivals, the various sects forget their differences and join together in the ceremonial prayer out of doors.

MOSLEM SECTS

Mohammed warned against divisions among his followers, saying "Take tight hold of God's rope all together and do not part in sects. You were enemies and God made friendship between your hearts and you are by His favor brothers." Yet he anticipated that divisions would come. According to tradition he said: "My people will be divided into seventy-three sects. Everyone of these sects will go to Hell except one." "Which one?" his companion asked, and Mohammed answered, "The religion which is professed by me and my companions."

The orthodox Moslems believe that they are this one chosen sect. They accept the Koran; they are Sunnites, for they follow the Sunna, the six books of traditions. They acknowledge all the Caliphs as rightful successors to Mohammed. They have four different schools of law, but their differences are not matters of principle, so all are acceptable. Mohammed said: "Differences of opinion in my community are a sign of the Divine Goodness."

Among the many heretical sects, the only one of permanent importance is that of the Shi'ites—separatists. They do not accept the Sunna, but have their own collection of traditions. They refuse to recognize the three Caliphs who preceded Ali, for he alone could carry on the Prophet's family line and Mohammed said, "The world will not come to an end before a man of my family, bearing my name, rises and leads my people."

The Shi'ites consider Ali and all his successors spiritual as well as political leaders. Since Ali and his two sons suffered violent deaths, the Shi'ites came to believe that their Imams must die as martyrs and through their suffering bring redemption to their followers. The twelfth Imam, who bore the name of Mohammed, disappeared while still a young man, leaving no son. The Shi'ites are sure that he is the leader whom the Prophet had promised, that he still lives, waiting until the right moment to usher in a new era of righteousness, liberty, and prosperity.

Shi'ites are a small minority in Islam; but in Persia, Shi'a is the state religion.

This dervish is a Shi'ite, as shown by his staff which carries the hand of Ali for protection and blessing. The begging bowl that he carries as a symbol of poverty is also used for eating and sometimes to protect his head from extreme heat.

THE DERVISH BROTHERHOODS

In every religion there are those who believe that they can best know and serve God by withdrawing from ordinary life, spending much time in meditation and prayer, and in repeating verses from their sacred writings. They put religion first in their lives and give up all worldly ambitions, living in monasteries or as wanderers. Christianity and Buddhism have monks and nuns. In Islam such persons are called fakirs—the Arabic word for poor. The Persian word is dervish.

Moslem monks are also called Sufis, probably because they wear garments of coarse woolen cloth, suf. Their belief that knowledge of God comes directly to the soul that loves Him above all else and waits patiently before Him is known as Sufism.

Very early, informal groups of Moslem ascetics gathered around some revered leader, who became their Sheik. In time the Sheiks established Orders with permanent homes and fixed rules of discipline and rituals of devotion.

Dervishes, like all oriental mystics, have learned that movement and controlled breathing increase the emotional response to the words repeated. The whole body worships; every motion has meaning for the initiated. Sometimes they work themselves into a frenzy or even unconsciousness, believing that "he knows God best who is most lost in Him."

Sufis have been popular missionaries. They tell stories which they have gathered from many sources, old Arab and Persian, Buddhist and Christian, fitting them into Islam as best they can. They have gone into the interior of Africa and as far as the East Indies and the Philippines. Everywhere the masses have responded; yet everywhere many phases of the old religions have lived on in the hearts and habits of the people.

Sufism has reached its highest development in Persia. The Persians are more poetic, more gentle, less warlike than the Arabs. Theirs is not so much a fighting faith as a contemplative one. They naturally express themselves in allegorical language and imaginative figures. The greatest poets of Persia have written of love, which for them symbolizes the oneness between God and the human soul, and their painters have portrayed love scenes which have spiritual meaning for one who understands. In this they show their kinship with those Hindus for whom the flute of Krishna is the call of God to the human soul.

WORLDWIDE ISLAM

Islam is more wide spread than any other religion except Christianity. It is still the dominant religion in the land of its birth and the neighboring countries and throughout central Asia. When Genghis Khan and his nomadic hordes descended upon western Asia, they were not Moslems, but when they went home they carried the religion with them to Mongolia and outer China. There are many Moslems in China today, especially in the western sections. These Moslems are largely Chinese in blood and are far from the center of their faith, but they are faithful in most of the observances. For example, many of them are butchers, but they never sell pork, though this is the favorite meat of China.

Malaya and Indonesia are Moslem lands. Early Arab men of the sea visited their shores and some settled there. The natives adopted many of the customs of their new neighbors. Later missionaries won the people to Islam, although many marks of Hinduism and Buddhism are still found there. Second only to India in the number of believers, these countries send the largest groups of pilgrims to the annual celebration in Mecca.

In the Philippines there are Moslems, known as Moros. They were the last Malayans to invade these islands and they brought their religion with them. They are a warlike people and have resisted the influence of both Spanish and American Christians.

The Balkan states and Russia are the only European countries which have any considerable number of Moslems in their population. Their presence dates back to the thirteenth century when the Mongols opened the way for Islam to the valley of the Danube and the shores of the Baltic. In Czarist Russia the Eastern Orthodox Church was the state religion and Moslems were at a disadvantage. When the Soviet regime overthrew both the monarchy and the church, it gave Moslems equal opportunities for education and economic advance and they responded with loyalty to the new government. They fought valiantly with Russia during World War II, quoting the Koran, "Do battle against those who raise the sword against you." In return the Kremlin has recognized their loyalty and has assisted them in building new mosques and given them permission to make the pilgrimage to Mecca. Those parts of western and central Asia which Soviet Russia now controls have a large Moslem population.

The imposing mosques of Istambul, built during the five hundred years when the Ottoman Turks were the leaders of Islam, stand as a symbol of the persistent hold of the religion upon the country. Turkey is fast becoming a western nation, but it is still a Moslem land.

This mosque was built by Sultan Ahmed in the seventeenth century. He worked on it with his own hands. The obelisk was brought from Egypt in the fourth century.

The Tower of Victory at Delhi, acclaimed "the most perfect tower in the world," was built in the early thirteenth century to commemorate the Moslem conquest of India. It is an outstanding example of Saracenic architecture.

ISLAM IN INDIA—PAKISTAN

Pakistan is the largest Moslem state in the world with a population of over eighty million—exceeded only by China, India, Russia, and the United States. The nation is based on religious unity, not oneness of race, language, or economic status. Its influence upon other Islamic countries will be far-reaching. Pakistan is the youngest Moslem state, separated in 1947 from India as the result of the long fierce struggle between Moslems and Hindus.

The first wave of Moslem invasion in the seventh century left no permanent results, but others did. The name which still rings in Asia and about which legend gathered is that of Sultan Mahmud of the eleventh century, who ruled Ghazna, the land between Persia and India. Seventeen times he came with his armies over the mountains into India and extended his empire as far east as the Ganges. He was more than a conqueror; he was also an ardent missionary of his faith. He destroyed Hindu temples and their idols in the name of Allah, the One and Only God, and won many converts. The next conquerors, from Afghanistan, were also Moslems, whose hold further strengthened the faith.

Timur, the dashing conqueror better known as Tamberlane—Timur the lame—made himself master of all of central Asia. In a hurried excursion into India, in 1398, he destroyed many villages, conquered Delhi, the capital, and returned home within three months. His rich spoils included ninety camels loaded with stones to build a mosque in his capital city of Samarkand. But he did not follow up his victories. That remained for Baber, who was his descendant in the fifth generation and also a descendant on his mother's side from Genghis Khan. At the head of Mongol armies, he extended the Moslem territory of India and founded the Mongul Empire, the first unified control of the land. However, it was not until the reign of his grandson, Akbar, that the emperor became the undisputed ruler of most of the country. Akbar was not only a brilliant warrior but also a wise and able administrator. He was a sage and a Sufi, tolerant in religion as mystics are apt to be. He did not destroy Hindu temples but allowed freedom of worship. He gathered about himself Hindu, Buddhist, and Christian priests. It is reported that he had one Hindu and one Christian among his wives.

Akbar had built his capital near Agra and in that city his grandson, Shah Jahan, a contemporary of Queen Elizabeth of England, erected the Taj Mahal. This mausoleum for his favorite wife, Mumtaz Mahal—the Elect of the Palace—is the most exquisite creation of Indian Moslem art. Shah Jahan also built the splendid fort and palace at Delhi.

The sixth and last of the "Great Moguls," as the Portuguese called them, was Aurangzeb, who extended his sway to the extreme south of India and built military highways to bind his empire together; he had fast runners to carry messages and bullock carts for trade. When he died in 1707 many Hindu communities declared their independence.

The days of the strength and glory of the Mogul Empire were over, though it survived in name until 1857, when the British Queen Victoria took over the government as Empress of India. For three hundred and thirty years Moslems had ruled India and had built up the only country-wide empire the land had ever known.

While Moslem armies were overrunning northern India, Portuguese traders found their way to the southeast coast. They were bent upon commerce conquest, and the conversion of the natives to the Christian faith of Rome. Their relations with the Indians were peaceful. But when the Moslem Empire extended its control into the region, both military conflict and antagonism between Islam and Christianity followed.

A little later, Dutch and British, Danes and Frenchmen vied with the Portuguese and with each other for the Indian trade. Soon wars in Europe led to struggles among the nationals of the warring countries who were in India. The collapse of the Mogul power brought further disorders to the unhappy land. All this came to a head in fighting between the British and the Moslems. To protect themselves and their investments and to restore order, the British took over the government, promising political and civil justice and religious tolerance.

For ninety years the British kept this promise, but there was growing demand on the part of the great majority of Indians for independence. They felt that at best the government was foreign, with little understanding of Indian traditions and customs and little adaptation to Indian conditions. It assumed that western ways were best and that it was a kindness to impose them upon India. The attitude was that of a well-wishing grandfather. Many questioned even the well-wishing, saying that the welfare of India was always subordinated to the advantage of Britain. "India is the richest jewel in the crown of Empire" was an irritating British boast.

The Taj Mahal is the most renowned building in India. It is surrounded by a garden, as were most tombs of the wealthy. Built of gleaming white marble, its inlays of jasper, porphyry, lapis lazuli, and serpentine are in delicate patterns of flowing arabesque, symbolic of the beauty, richness, harmony, and endlessness of love.

The latticed screen of white marble surrounds the tombs. Its intricate filigree is a miracle of delicate workmanship.

Enclosed by the octagonal screen rest the cenotaphs of Mumtaz Mahal and her husband, Shah Jahan. The marble surfaces are covered with floral designs and decorative inscriptions from the Koran.

The critics of British policy presented evidence that the administration was ready to encourage divisions and disorder to strengthen its own hold upon the country. It was the British viceroy who first made a political division on the basis of religious "communities," thus emphasizing the differences between Hindus and Moslems. Appointments to office, admission to the higher schools, positions in the army were made on the basis of proportional representation of the two groups. Elections were on the same basis, so that a person's religion determined his political party. Even though Hindus and Moslems might be close neighbors, they belonged to different communities; each community was a closely knit unit however widely scattered or however different in other respects its members might be. This is what is known as communalism. Jealousies and suspicions between the two groups led to bitter antagonism and deadly rivalry.

At times Hindus and Moslems forgot their enmities in order to unite in the struggle for freedom. But ever and again the communal spirit flared up; riots and disorders arose which gave the British ground for saying that they could not withdraw until there was unity and agreement.

The antagonism of the Moslems toward the Hindus is the result in part of a curious combination of a sense of inferiority and a consciousness of superiority. They are fewer in number, only about a third as many in the country as a whole though in certain sections they are in the majority. The present day Moslems do not differ from their Hindu countrymen in race or blood. Only about ten per cent of them are descended from the Moslem invaders and most of those have only one foreign ancestor among many who were Indian nationals. Yet they are more backward in education. The reasons for this are not hard to understand. The early converts to Islam in India, as later the first converts to Christianity, were largely from the poor and oppressed classes to whom Islam's message of brotherhood was a message of real deliverance. The first European contacts were in the south and only gradually reached the northwest where most of the Moslems are.

In any society, a group which is smaller in numbers and retarded in development finds itself dominated by the larger and more advanced group. This is strikingly apparent in the condition of American negroes. It is not strange therefore that most Moslems saw in the free democracy promised by Britain to a united India the threat of perpetual Hindu domination. They preferred communalism and even felt that their interests were better protected by the presence of the British. "A brown elephant is not better than a white one," they said.

Moslem national feeling ran high in the communal prayers of the main festivals, at which the Imam prayed for the coming of the Moslem state. On the Feast of the Breaking of the Fast, friends embrace each other in oriental style.

A Hindu shrine like this was often the cause of street riots, for to the Moslem every idol is a rival to the one true God.

The knowledge that they had less influence in the country than the Hindus was particularly galling to the Moslems because of their sense of superiority. They are sure that Allah is the only God and Islam the one true religion. They know that it has been the civilizing and unifying force over vast areas of the world. More than that, Mohammed taught that his people of whatever races or lands are a community; therefore they believe that they should be free to preserve their own ideals and way of life in a community of their own.

The Hindus in turn resent the Moslems as outsiders, even though only a small proportion of them are descendants of invaders from the west. They remember the brutality and ruthless destruction of the Moslem invasions and contrast the Hindu teaching of non-injury. They resent especially that the conquerors showed no respect for their sacred places but tore down their temples and the images of their gods. When the Moslems undertook to purify their religion by removing the Hindu elements which had crept into it, the Hindus considered it an additional insult; the breach between the two groups widened.

Street riots have started from small incidents. A Moslem, to whom every idol seems a rival of the one true God, dishonors in some way the image of a Hindu wayside shrine and is attacked by Hindus. A procession with music passes a mosque during the hour of prayer and the Moslems, whom Mohammed taught to think of music as "the muezzin of the devil," break up the procession. A Hindu's indignation rises when he passes a market where beef is sold, for to Hindus the cow is sacred. The Moslem is repeatedly humiliated when the high caste Hindu draws his garments closely about him as he passes lest he be contaminated by contact with a non-Hindu, for to the strict Hindu all non-Hindus are outside the pale.

Most serious disorders spring from economic injustices, Moslem peasants rising against their Hindu landlords or workmen against their Hindu overseers. If a Moslem employer is unfair to Moslem labor, the individual is called an oppressor and that is all. But if a Hindu employer is unfair, the cry goes up that Hindus are oppressing Moslems; nationalism flares, religion is invoked, passion rises to white heat. Often blood is shed before the police can restore order. Resentment and hatred on both sides have grown more bitter.

Hindus often accused the Moslems of being only halfhearted in the struggle for self-rule for India, and of putting the welfare of their own community above that of the country as a whole. There was some truth in this. Yet many of the most enlightened and prosperous Moslems worked hard in the cause of a united India with complete separation between political and religious matters.

In 1885 the Indian National Congress was organized, the most important and representative political organization in India; it included Moslems. In 1937 it won the elections in most of the provinces.

The Moslem League, which was organized in 1906, at first cooperated with Congress in efforts for a self-governing India. But it wished to be considered the representative of all Moslems and to treat with Congress on equal terms; Congress refused this as there were many Moslems in its own organization. And so in 1933, the League launched a campaign in favor of a separate Moslem state in India, to be known as Pakistan—the Holy Land.

Pakistan became the dream utopia of its Moslem advocates, each picturing it according to his own ideals. They planned for economic, social, and cultural progress in a state which should be their own and to which they might give unqualified loyalty and service.

On August 15, 1947, Pakistan was born by agreement with the Hindus and with the full cooperation of Britain. The new nation was quickly recognized by other nations and admitted into the United Nations. In the northwestern part of India the population is predominantly Moslem. Elsewhere the Moslem population is so widely scattered that fixing the borders between Pakistan and Hindu India involved many difficulties, particularly in states where the ruler was of one religion and the majority of the population of the other. Some eight to ten million people migrated, Moslems from Hindu territory, Hindus from Moslem. Even so the population is still mixed. The misery involved in such uprooting and disrupting of normal economic life was appalling. Religious and communal frenzy led to riots and intensified the sufferings. Yet less than three per cent of the population of India was involved and the period of violence in most sections was brief. The long time problems of poverty and disease, of resettlement, housing, and employment, will test severely the leaders and people of both of the new states. In addition, Pakistan wrestles with the creation of an entirely new state, in which the ancient laws and ideals of Islam shall regulate a modern society.

In the new nation of Pakistan, girls as well as boys are given education and are trained for useful citizenship.

Jerusalem, Holy City of three faiths.

ISLAM IN PALESTINE

Palestine is the Holy Land of three faiths. Here the Hebrew nation established itself and made Jerusalem the "City of the Great King"—God Himself. The Jews, scattered over the world for two thousand years, have continued to look to it as their home land. Here Jesus lived his brief earthly life. Here, according to Moslem tradition, Mohammed was brought by the angel Gabriel. Here in the seventh century a Moslem conqueror built the sacred shrine, the Dome of the Rock.

In Palestine, as in India, rival claims have made the land a trouble spot. In each case, one party is Moslem. In each, Moslems are more backward in economic and cultural development. But here the similarity ends. India is a vast country, about half the size of the United States, isolated from the rest of the world by seas and mountains. Palestine is small, about the size of the state of Vermont. This little country has been, through all its history, the bridge connecting countries larger and stronger than itself; across it trade-caravans have traveled and armies have marched. Its fortunes are of concern to many nations.

In India, the basis for the division between Moslems and Hindus is religious; in Palestine, the basis is racial, between Arabs and Jews, for there is a considerable number of Christians among the Arabs and national existence rather than religion is the primary concern of the Jews. The similarities between the faith of the Jews and the daughter religion, Islam, are so great that neither one offends the other seriously. In India, the Moslems are outnumbered, three to one, by the Hindus; in Palestine, Arabs have outnumbered their rivals, the Jews, two to one. In India, Moslems want a land which they can call their own and where they can develop their own culture; in Palestine Jews ask the same thing. In India, Moslems favored cummunalism and segregation, fearing perpetual domination by the Hindu majority in a united country; in Palestine, Jews favored division for similar reasons, while Arabs opposed it.

During World War I Britain needed help to guard her highway of Empire. She negotiated secretly with the Arabs, whose several countries were then part of the Turkish Empire. She promised independence after the hoped-for Allied victory in return for permission to move up from Egypt against Turkey through their lands. Britain also sought the help of Jews everywhere, promising to support their effort to establish in Palestine "a national home for the Jewish people." This is the historic Declaration of Lord Balfour, then Foreign Secretary. After the war Britain became the administering power.

The Jews, or Hebrews to use the ancient name, have considered Palestine their home country ever since Moses brought them to the borders of the land. They never relinquished their claim to the land which God promised to their fathers. Did not the prophet write: "The Lord shall set His hand to restore the remnants of His people, and He shall gather together the depressed of Judah from the four corners of the earth?"

Every Friday, century after century, Jews have prayed with their faces against the mighty stone wall of the temple court now in the hands of Moslems which they are forbidden to enter. They have chanted the ancient lament, "Our greatness is departed. How long, O Lord, how long?" And in every land, Jews sing the modern anthem of faith, "Yet is our hope not lost, our ancient hope, to dwell in the land of our fathers."

This hope is the foundation of Zionism, a movement started in 1897 and greatly strengthened by the Balfour Declaration. Thousands of Jews of eastern Europe have colonized the land and planted fields, gardens and orchards. More fortunate Jews in prosperous lands have contributed millions of dollars to develop industries and irrigation and power systems, and to establish hospitals, schools, libraries, and a university. The standard of living for the entire country has been raised.

Arabs, too, were attracted to the prospering land; tribes that had been living the primitive nomad life came in to settle and to work on roads or construction projects. Babies that would have died under old conditions lived to grow up because of modern sanitation and medical care. The total population more than doubled in thirty years. Questions of ownership and control became difficult.

The need of a Jewish state was intensified by the frightful sufferings of Jews in Europe during and after the second World War. The Jews of Palestine were eager to receive them and to give them a new hope; the Jews of America were ready to help finance them. But the Arabs thought they should have the right to say how many refugees should come into their land; they could not understand why larger nations, unwilling to open their own doors, should urge Palestine to provide sanctuary. They feared that the Jewish population would become the majority; the Jews hoped for exactly that, for they had nationalist motives as well as those of pity. Immigration became the primary problem. When Britain allowed it, the Arabs protested; when she restricted it, the Jews tried to smuggle in the poor unfortunates.

*The future of Islam should be secure in the hands of alert and educated
boys like these.*

Britain asked the United Nations to take over the problem. After careful study the Special Committee recommended partition of the land into two states, Arab and Jewish, bound together in an economic union.

In contrast to India, where plans for partition were worked out with full cooperation of the two states and Britain, the partition of Palestine was imposed upon the land by an external authority. Why, asked the Arabs, should they alone have no right of self-determination? They have the suspicion that their welfare was a secondary consideration with states which thought first of how the decisions would affect their own national interests, and even by politicians who considered the effect upon elections.

Islam has had defeats as well as victories in its thirteen centuries of history; it has been forced to surrender some of its conquests; but it has never yielded native soil. To the Arab world, Palestine is "native soil." When the armies of Islam took it, they took it from the Romans, not from the Jews, who had lost their control long before. It was already sacred land to the Moslems because Mohammed had visited it. They loved every foot of it as all people love what has been the home of their fathers for hundreds of years. True, Arab Palestine has never been an independent state, but Arabs have constituted most of its population and it has been a part of Moslem empires. True also that the Arabs never developed the land as the Jews have done, but they did not have the wealth of America upon which to draw and they had suffered from many wars and the exploitation of their overlords. With larger freedom and more education, they would have liked the opportunity to work out their own salvation.

In their protest against partition, the Arabs of Palestine had the support of the six neighbor Arab states. These were granted the independence promised at the time of World War I; they are making rapid strides in self-development; they are members of the United Nations. They do not like the idea of a state of different nationality, culture, and customs set down in the midst of Arab land. But one by one they accepted the inevitable and signed treaties with Israel.

In the controversy between Arabs and Jews there was no call to a Holy War, but the neighboring states shared in the bitter fighting in varying degrees. King 'Abd-allah of Transjordan was the most aggressive leader and succeeded in occupying the section of Jerusalem which was the ancient city. Later, he took over the administration of Arab central Palestine, changed the name of his kingdom to Jordan, and in 1950, formally annexed the Arab Palestine territory. This increased jealousies among the Arab states as well as fear of Israel. In spite of the efforts of the United Nations, final adjustment of the intra-Arab tensions and the conflicting interests of Arabs and Israelis may be long delayed.

Saudi Arabia, one of Palestine's neighboring states, is intent upon raising its standard of living. The workers on this experimental farm are utilizing irrigation and other scientific methods of agriculture in a hot dry land.

ISLAM IN THE MODERN WORLD

The desert, that for centuries knew only camel-trains, is now crossed by auto-highways, railroads, and air routes. Yet in spite of all the changes of the modern world, life and religion for the vast majority of Moslems are what they were a millennium ago. They tend their flocks and fields as their fathers have for centuries. But even for them war and the radio have brought some contact with modern movements.

Some of those who are most conscious that the world is different resist the change; others welcome it. The orthodox who take every word of the Koran literally are most concerned with preserving the past. It is enough for them that Mohammed has spoken. To them he left the defense of the Faith. They believe the first step in defense is to free Islam from all modern innovations. The most extreme conservatives have gone back to the desert in the attempt to live again the simple life of early Islam. Others try to maintain the ancient ways in the midst of the modern world.

Progressive Moslems, especially in Egypt, Turkey, and Pakistan, are ready to modernize Islam. They know that it cannot be universal and broadly democratic unless it is a growing faith. They claim the right to think freely, but recognize that "human reason must humble itself before God." They are alert for modern knowledge, but insist that change should come, not from imitation of the materialistic West, but by development from within; necessary changes, they say, are not contrary to the spirit of Islam. They have adopted western dress. They are working to raise the standard of living as a better way of dealing with poverty than the traditional alms-giving. They have made slavery unlawful and oppose polygamy and easy divorce. They encourage the education of women and wish them to share social and civic responsibilities.

A hundred years ago in Persia, an upsurge of intense religious conviction led to the birth of the Baha'i World Faith. First regarded as a Shi'ite sect, it has established itself as an independent world-religion. Its members belong to more than thirty races and live in some ninety countries; they have come from all the great religions and from no religion. Baha'i acknowledges its debt to Islam, but it also accepts the truth made known in other revealed religions. This daughter religion may prove to be a significant contribution of Islam to the modern world.

Part of the mission which Mohammed saw before him was uniting the hostile tribes of Arabia in a common faith in One God and in a common loyalty to their community. The accomplishment of Islam has gone far beyond his dreams.

One of the reasons for this rapid spread of Islam has been its simplicity and directness. It has no priesthood, no mystical sacraments, no elaborate doctrines. Its duties are definite and practical, its standards attainable by the average person, its hopes popular.

The democracy of Islam is like the democracy of an army. There is no place for petty distinctions among men who bow in submission before the Supreme Ruler. Each human soul has significance, for he comes directly into God's presence five times a day. No man may despise one to whom the Almighty gives ear. The discipline of Islam is the same for all. The requirements may be adapted to conditions, but there are no personal exceptions. "It is commanded" is the final word; "At Thy bidding" the universal response.

Moslems hold that Islam can unite the world. They believe that it can give man what he most wants—a sense of personal worth, the consciousness of God, and the challenge of submission to Him and devotion to His cause; that it can give the world what is most needs—brotherhood above the strife of rival sects, the conflicts of races and classes, the struggle of individuals and nations for supremacy.

East and West are meeting in the modern world. Islam belongs to both. Far-sighted leaders believe its mission is to combine the insights of East and West and stimulate the richer life which comes from the meeting of diverse cultures.

Under stress of dangers and opportunities, awakened Islam has new appreciation of its own genius and a sense of obligation to share its universal message. It offers itself as the last of the great religions, the religion for all mankind.

London Mosque showing Crescent.

PHOTOGRAPHS

INDEX